SO THEREFORE ...

Every scene or action or speech has a *so therefore*. It is the goal, the ultimate statement of the character. You should know the *so therefore* as you begin your scene ... The climax and the payoff is the *so therefore*.

from Al Ruscio's preface

When working through a scene with a student, renowned actor and acting teacher Al Ruscio will ask, "so therefore what?" to urge them to capture the specific actions and desires that define their character at that moment. *So Therefore* ... interweaves tried-and-tested practical exercises with sound advice, and illustrative tales from Ruscio's remarkable career, to form a training handbook as uniquely pragmatic as his favourite phrase. Breaking down his method into three broad focuses, Ruscio considers:

- *Warming up* – including relaxation, going "beneath the words" and emotional recall;
- *Scene work* – ranging from character analysis to an exploration of action;
- *The play* – discovering its spine, progressing through rehearsals, and sustaining a performance.

But *So Therefore* ... also reflects wisely on such diverse subjects as "stage versus film," and "stamina, luck and chutzpah." Enriching and generous, it is the culmination of a career that has taken in dozens of major motion pictures, and spans the entire history of television – as well as half a century spent training actors.

Al Ruscio graduated from the famed Neighborhood Playhouse School of the Theatre and has been teaching acting for five decades. He has served on the Board of Directors of the Screen Actors Guild and is a current voting member of the Academy of Motion Picture Arts and Sciences.

SO THEREFORE ...

A PRACTICAL GUIDE FOR ACTORS

Al Ruscio

Routledge
Taylor & Francis Group

LONDON AND NEW YORK

754734682

First published 2012
by Routledge
2 Park Square, Milton Park, Abingdon, Oxon OX14 4RN

Simultaneously published in the USA and Canada
by Routledge
711 Third Avenue, New York, NY 10017

Routledge is an imprint of the Taylor & Francis Group, an informa business

British Library Cataloguing in publication data
A catalogue record for this book is available from the British Library

Library of Congress Cataloguing in publication data
Ruscio, Al, 1924–
So therefore : a practical guide for actors / by Al Ruscio.
    p. cm.
    Includes bibliographical references and index.
    1. Acting. I. Title.
    PN2061.R74 2012   792.02'8--dc23
    2011052606

ISBN: 978-0-415-51671-6 (hbk)
ISBN: 978-0-415-51672-3 (pbk)
ISBN: 978-0-203-12405-5 (ebk)

Typeset in Garamond Pro and Gill Sans
by Bookcraft Limited, Stroud, Gloucestershire

Printed and bound in Great Britain by the MPG Books Group

I dedicate this book to four remarkable teachers who helped me, guided me, and inspired me along the way. To John Tellier, at Salem High School in Massachusetts, who taught me never to be afraid. To Dr. Delbert Moyer Staley, of Staley College of the Spoken Word in Massachusetts, who gave me my first opportunity to teach a class. To Sanford Meisner, at the Neighborhood Playhouse School of the Theatre in New York City, who taught me the fundamentals of acting. And to Jeff Corey, in Los Angeles, who shared his teaching skills and expanded my approach to the craft of acting.

CONTENTS

PART 3
The play   75

PART 4
Stage versus film   111

PART 5
Stamina, luck, and chutzpah, and other lessons   123

FIGURES

FOREWORD

Martin Landau

I just had the pleasure of reading Al Ruscio's *So Therefore …* I found it an absolute joy on many levels. It's not only a great primer on the art of acting in theatre and film, but it allows the reader a close-up view of the author, a devoted and talented man whose own life's journey has instilled knowledge and given incentive to so many others over the years.

I have known Al Ruscio for over a half century, and I can honestly say that his talent and zeal have not diminished even one iota in all that time.

Al is an enlightened individual with a true and passionate love of life and his craft – and it's bursting from the pages of this book.

I recommend it highly to everyone, not only actors or those involved in theatre and film – *everyone* – as it will give the reader insights and stimulate him or her in ways which will improve how they look at and experience the world around them. *It's a terrific read!*

PREFACE
SO THEREFORE ... (A FEW WORDS ABOUT MY TITLE)

I did not invent the phrase "so therefore", but I used it so often in my classes that my students would use the phrase whenever they would call me or see me after a class.

I believe I first heard the phrase in Sandy Meisner's class at the Neighborhood Playhouse in New York. After you finished a scene or a monologue or an exercise, he would say, "So therefore, what?" and you had to be specific in your answer.

For example, in the play *Golden Boy* by Clifford Odets, the boy is trying to explain to his family, especially his father, that he wants more from life: "Poppa, I have to tell you," he says, "I don't like myself – past, present and future. Do you know there are men who have wonderful things from life? Do you think they're better than me?" Then he continues, "Tomorrow's my birthday! I change my life."[1] And, I would say, "So therefore, what?" And the student would yell, "So therefore, leave me alone: I'm going to be a fighter." Or in the play *Spoon River Anthology* by Edgar Lee Masters, when Lucinda Matlock talks about her great life and then says, "What is this I hear of sorrow and weariness, anger, discontent and drooping hopes? Degenerate sons and daughters," she says, "Life is too strong for you – it takes life to love Life."[2]

Her *so therefore* is something like, "Stop complaining, grow up, and enjoy this wonderful gift called Life."

Every scene or action or speech has a *so therefore*. It is the goal, the ultimate statement of the character. You should know the *so therefore* as you begin your scene. That knowledge is the springboard that drives the scene. It gives you the impetus and the confidence to play your action fully. The climax and the payoff is the *so therefore*.

ACKNOWLEDGMENTS

Putting this book together was truly a family affair. I want to thank my wife Kate Williamson for her love and encouragement. We met years ago as two struggling actors in New York and together we've had a fantastic journey that continues to this day.

I also thank our daughter Maria and her husband David Seward for their help and excellent suggestions. I thank our son-in-law Leon Martell. He has used this book in his own classes and he has given me great insight, especially regarding the exercises.

I thank our son Michael, an editor and director, for his help, particularly on Part 4, regarding film and stage acting, the editing process, and how it affects the actor.

I thank our daughter Nina, who used her knowledge of production design, and her husband Franz Metcalf, a published author, for organizing and editing this material.

I would be remiss if I didn't recognize the contributions and love and understanding of my agent-manager Judy Fox who was always there to do anything she could to help make this book successful.

Finally, I want to acknowledge and thank our daughter Elizabeth for her extraordinary effort in typing the entire manuscript and offering editorial and research assistance throughout the writing and rewriting process.

PERMISSIONS

ABOUT THE AUTHOR

Al Ruscio was born in Salem, Massachusetts, and began his theatrical career in earnest after serving in the Army Air Corps during World War II. While attending Staley College of the Spoken Word during the day, he acted with the New England Shakespeare Festival at night, playing Edgar in *King Lear*, Antonio in *The Merchant of Venice*, and Lucifer in *Dr. Faustus*.

The following summer, he joined the North Shore Players where he played roles in *Dream Girl* with Lucille Ball, *Burlesque* with Bert Lahr, and *Angel Street* with Francis Lederer. The summer after, he was playing leads opposite Martha Scott in *The Barretts of Wimpole Street*, Elissa Landi in *Theatre*, and Robert Alda in *The Male Animal*.

During his senior year in college he was invited to teach a course called Psycho-Gymnastics. This was a class in movement and gesture designed to help priests, ministers, rabbis, and politicians. Among his students, a future United States president: John F. Kennedy.

That same year, he was selected by director Henry Hathaway to appear in the film *13 Rue Madeleine*, with James Cagney and Richard Conte. It was Conte who suggested that Al study in New York. After graduating from college, and armed with Conte's recommendation, Al was accepted at the famed Neighborhood Playhouse School of the Theatre. He studied there for two years with Sanford Meisner, David Pressman, Martha Graham, and a host of wonderful teachers in acting, improvisation, dance, speech, production, and technique.

He then began teaching a class called Acting – The Professional Approach at Brooklyn College. At that time he also started to work in live television, appearing in episodes of *Kraft Television Theatre*,

Lux Video Theatre, and *Robert Montgomery Presents*. During the summers, he acted in summer stock in a variety of theatres in Maine, New Hampshire, New York, and Pennsylvania. Outstanding experiences were touring with Kim Stanley in *The Country Girl*, with Steve McQueen in *A Hatful of Rain*, with Gertrude Berg in *Arsenic and Old Lace*, and playing Max Levene in the road company of *Heaven Can Wait*.

Shortly after he arrived in Hollywood, Al starred in *A View from the Bridge* at the Players Ring Theatre. He also began to play major roles in *Bonanza*, *Mr. Lucky*, *The Untouchables*, *Playhouse 90*, and *The Lawless Years*. He appeared in the film *Al Capone* with Rod Steiger.

He began touring in George Bernard Shaw's *Don Juan in Hell*, playing the role of the Devil. During this time he was serving on the board of directors of the Screen Actors Guild. Jack Dales, the executive director of the Guild, suggested Al might be interested in a position at a new school just opening in Iowa: Midwestern College, in the small town of Denison. The position was Actor-in-Residence, Chairman of the Theatre Department, and Managing Director of the Fine Arts Festival.

Al accepted the challenge and for five years he taught acting and theatre history. He also acted, directed, or produced some 25 plays, including *Darkness at Noon*, *The Lark*, *The Caine Mutiny Court-Martial*, *The Music Man*, *Of Mice and Men*, *Barefoot in the Park*, and *The Seagull*. Unfortunately, the college closed after five years, but Al and everyone else involved will treasure that great adventure for the rest of their lives.

The University of Windsor then beckoned. Al and his family moved to Canada where he acted in or directed *Three Men on a Horse*, *J. B.*, *The Gingerbread Lady*, and *Leaving Home*. While acting and directing, he taught classes in improvisation and acting technique.

He was then invited to serve as artistic director at The Academy of Dramatic Art, Oakland University's professional acting school in Rochester, Michigan. There he directed *Look Homeward, Angel*, *The Long Voyage Home*, *The Green Cockatoo*, *After the Fall*, *J. B.*, *A View from the Bridge*, and four one-acts by Tennessee Williams. During this time in the middle of the country he also appeared as an actor in *Fever Heat*, as well as in several industrial films for Ford and General Motors.

He then returned to California and proceeded to become one of Hollywood's busiest character actors, racking up hundreds of guest star appearances as well as regular recurring roles on several classic television series. The list of Al's roles, which virtually spans all of television history, picks up in the mid-seventies with guest appearances on *The Rockford Files*, *One Day at a Time*, and *Starsky & Hutch*, and with a regular recurring role on *Lou Grant* as Carmine Rossi, a recovering alcoholic. In *Shannon* he played opposite Kevin Dobson, as his fisherman father-in-law. Next he starred in *Steambath* for Showtime as DaVinci, a cigar-smoking, towel-wearing, fun-loving character. In the eighties, he had major roles in several series: on *St. Elsewhere* as Rawley Moreland, an outspoken maintenance supervisor; on *Barney Miller* he played five different characters over its five-year run; and, on *Hill Street Blues*, four more. He also made multiple appearances on these eighties' shows: *Night Court*, *Cagney & Lacey*, and *Scarecrow and Mrs. King*.

From 1989 to 1993 Al played the warm, opera-loving grandfather on *Life Goes On*. The following year, he was a regular on *Joe's Life*, playing the wise-cracking waiter Frank. In addition, he appeared on these classic shows: *Seinfeld* (in the famous pilot, playing the restaurant manager), *Mad about You*, *The Wonder Years*, *ER*, and *NYPD Blue*. He played Otto Cornowitz opposite Tracey Ullman in *Tracey Takes On … Age*. On *Seventh Heaven*, his character Fred Fleming gets married off. Cult fans will appreciate his appearances as Elder Number Four on *The X-Files*. Soap opera fans will likewise appreciate his character Kosta Kanelos on *Port Charles*. Most recently, he appeared in the comedies *Malcolm & Eddie*, and *'Til Death*.

His film work also contains classics (besides the aforementioned *Al Capone*), most notably *Godfather III*, as the ill-fated fellow mobster Leo Cuneo; and the notorious *Showgirls*, where he plays the casino owner and gets to keep his clothes on. Other films include *Any Which Way You Can* with Clint Eastwood, *Romero* with Raul Julia, *Guilty by Suspicion* with Robert DeNiro, *Cage*, *Deadly Force*, *I Don't Buy Kisses Anymore*, and *The Phantom*. Al is a member of the Academy of Motion Pictures Arts and Sciences.

Al has also managed, over the years, to appear regularly on the Los Angeles legitimate stage. He played Mizlansky in *Mizlansky-Zilinsky*, Jon Robin Baitz's first play, and won the LA Weekly Award for his performance. He played Bart Keely in *Geniuses* at The Coronet. He won Drama-Logue Awards for his performances in *They Knew What They Wanted* and *The Man in the Glass Booth*. He was standby for Jack Lemmon in *Tribute*, guest starred as Shylock in *The Merchant of Venice* at the University of California in Santa Barbara, played Maurice in the world premiere of *The Geography of Luck* at the South Coast Repertory Theatre, Bernie Ludd in *The Soliloquy of Bernie Ludd* at the Actors Studio West, and Judah Prince in *Rocket to the Moon*.

Throughout this entire time he also taught master classes in acting, beginning with his association with veteran acting teacher and fellow actor, the late Jeff Corey. He shared a teaching studio with Jeff, as well as a long and fruitful teaching relationship.

His exceptional turn as King Lear at the University of California in Santa Barbara, a production which gets a heartfelt treatment in this book, was rewarded with these reviews: "This *King Lear* is quite simply the finest production of a Shakespeare play I've ever seen … Ruscio gives a mesmerizing performance,"[1] and "The role of Lear is the supreme test of a mature actor's craft and guest artist Al Ruscio, a familiar face from film and television, rises magnificently to the challenge."[2]

For the past twenty years, Al and his wife, actress Kate Williamson, have conducted acting workshops specifically designed for animators. Prompted by Al's acting student, highly regarded animator Glen Keane, and championed by Bill Matthews, former head of artistic training for Disney Studios' feature animation department, Al and Kate pioneered their techniques with animators at Warner Brothers Studios; Walt Disney Studios in Burbank, California and Orlando, Florida; Rhythm and Hues in Los Angeles; and Pixar Studios, along with numerous other animation houses.

Most recently Al has wrapped production on the Forrest Whitaker feature *Winged Creatures*. Al continues to act, write, and teach with no intention of retiring.

Part I

WARMING UP

1

INTRODUCTION

We begin with this section called *Warming up*. It sets out some exercises for you to do. These exercises are like theatre games. They are fun and they are basic. They provide the foundation of our work.

You will learn how to relax so that you can focus and begin to imagine. Then, you will work on sensory problems to help you fully see and hear and smell and touch and taste. Then, on to improvisation and the study of people and animals. Finally, you will work on emotional memory exercises.

All of this work is intended to prepare you for scene work and character study. By the time you are finished with Part 1, you will be warmed up and ready for Part 2.

The exercises and their aims

Relaxation: to free the actor of tension
Concentration: to help the actor learn to direct his or her focus
Imagination: to allow pictures in the mind to soar
Beneath the words: to think as the character

* Subtext: to explore what is really happening beneath the words
* Inner monologue: to explore what you are thinking when not speaking and during pauses when you are speaking

Sensory exercises: to develop a heightened sense of awareness
Improvisation: to open up your natural instincts through the use of freewheeling exercises

Animal studies: to observe and study all kinds of animal behavior for use as you explore characters

Life studies: to recognize that the world is your classroom and the things you have seen, known, and experienced, and the people you have met and studied, are unique to you

Emotional recall: to understand how deeply personal and intimate experiences can heighten, enrich, and illuminate your work

2

RELAXATION

Tension is misplaced energy. When there is tension in a body, one cannot think or feel.[1]

Lee Strasberg

Tension is the enemy of relaxation. It is the occupational disease of the actor. It can destroy your concentration, or cause you to lose focus and to wander on stage or in front of the camera. It must be searched out, discovered, and released to free you for your work as an actor.

The following exercises will help you achieve relaxation. They can be done at home alone or in groups under the guidance of a coach. They can be done before rehearsals or in class or before a performance.

Relaxation exercises

- Face a wall. Pretend you are a cat on a lazy summer afternoon. Slowly stretch against the wall. In slow motion, literally climb the wall. Extend your fingers as high as you can. Stand tiptoe. Stretch one arm at a time in a swimming motion. Then yawn and shake all over. Shake your arms and legs. Enjoy making exaggerated chewing sounds and noises.
- Sitting in a chair, close your eyes. Listen to the sounds in the room. Listen to the sounds in the street. Try to hear distinct sounds, voices, etc. Now, with your fingers, check the major points of tension in your body: the temples, the mouth, the jaw, the eyes, the bridge of the nose, the arms, the fingers, the shoulders. Focus

on the areas where you feel there is some tension. Now drop your head forward and imagine you are a huge dead weight. Let the weight carry you forward until you lie in a heap on the floor. Lie on your back. Now stretch and yawn. Make yourself as large as possible. Cover as much ground as you can. As you yawn and stretch repeat the phrase, "Oh, yes." Enjoy the sense of freedom.

- Stand comfortably and relaxed. Pretend to walk into a pool of water. The water is tension. Imagine the water slowly climbing up onto you. Start with your toes. Tense your toes, imagining the water is tension. Hold that. Now your heels. Hold that. Now your entire foot. Retaining the tension in your foot, slowly apply tension to your ankles, then up through your legs into your calves, knees, upper legs, hips, abdomen, and the base of your spine. Then up through your body, your shoulders, elbows, and fists. Clench each finger. Now your chest, jaw, teeth, cheeks, lips, ears, forehead, and the top of your head. Lastly, your eyes. Now you should be completely covered with water, with tension. Focus on a point directly in front of you. Tense your entire body, then let go of the tension. Slowly collapse into a heap. Yawn and stretch.
- Stand with your feet comfortably apart. Drop your head onto your chest as if it is a huge weight, like a cannon ball. Slowly move your head onto your left shoulder. Your mouth should be open, your jaw relaxed, limp. The weight of your head should make it flop straight back. Slowly, flop your head onto your right shoulder. Then move your head down to the original position. Remember, your head is heavy and its weight is what makes it move. Do not make it happen, *allow* it to happen. As you repeat the exercise, yawn. Feel the back of your throat open up. Now stretch and make yourself as tall as possible. Shake all over until you begin to feel like a rag doll. Now, slowly sit down and try to retain that sense of ease and freedom.

The purpose of relaxation is to allow you to work with your body, your mind, and your spirit, free of tension.

3

CONCENTRATION

Remember this word *Concentrate*. Concentration is the quality which permits us to direct all our spiritual and intellectual forces towards one definite object and to continue as long as it pleases us to do so. This strength, this certainty of power over yourself, is the fundamental quality of every creative artist. You must find it within yourself, and develop it to the last degree.[1]

Richard Boleslavsky

Concentration must be approached affirmatively, that is, you must believe with all your being in the thing you are doing. It must have reality and substance for you. Too many times, actors will attempt to block out everything else. It is more rewarding to give yourself completely to the object of your concentration.

Though you may perform these exercises by yourself, it would be more beneficial if they were done in a classroom situation with a leader who could then comment on the work.

Concentration exercises

- Choose a small object and concentrate on it. Others should try to distract you and break your concentration.
- Fix a thought in your mind. Give yourself to it, really focus on it. Other students (one or two at a time) should try to distract you.
- Pick a subject with which you are familiar. Begin to talk to a group about this subject. Give the group a life (they are stockholders in

a company, they are fellow students and wish to complain about meals, the tuition, etc.). They should try to distract you with noise, other talk, etc. They may even try to heckle you.

- Recite the alphabet, first forwards and then backwards. Try reciting with distractions.
- Put on sad music and talk about something happy. Then put on happy music and talk about something sad.
- Read the description of a set at the beginning of a play. Read it aloud. People should quiz you about the contents to see if you really were concentrating on the material.
- Listen to an orchestra and pick out a single instrument. Concentrate on it.
- Relate, through using only one sense, an unusual experience that has happened to you.
- Concentrate on one sense each day. Bring and relate your sensory experiences to class. On Monday, you could do an exercise using only the sense of taste; on Tuesday, the sense of smell; on Wednesday, the sense of touch; on Thursday, the sense of sight; on Friday, the sense of hearing. This has the elements of a game. On Monday, you will say, "I will really taste everything today and then bring that taste to the class. I will recreate the experience and sharpen my senses."
- Before retiring at night, focus on your day. Try to retrace your steps. Go through what you ate, where you went, what you did, paying particular attention to any unusual sensory or emotional experiences that affected you deeply. Be specific and try to bring back the images in detail.

A note on concentration

I learned my lesson in concentration early in my career. I had the good fortune to be selected by director Henry Hathaway to play an OSS (Office of Strategic Services) student in a 20th Century Fox film called *13 Rue Madeleine*. It starred James Cagney.

I remembered Mr. Cagney from his early films *Public Enemy*, *The Roaring Twenties*, and *Angels with Dirty Faces*, but in this film he showed me an entirely different side of his talent. He was playing a group leader about to begin a dangerous mission and, in this scene, was outlining our tasks and the danger of the operation.

Mr. Cagney had a long monologue in which he was describing the nature of our mission and the necessity for timing and cooperation. He stood at the top of the staircase and slowly walked down towards us. The camera operator was on a crane, following him from the top of the staircase to the bottom where we were standing and listening to his directions.

We began the scene very early in the morning. Mr. Cagney would begin his speech, then stop, go back to the top of the stairs and begin again. Sometimes, the director would stop and say something, but more often than not, Mr. Cagney would stop himself and say things like, "I can do it better," or "Don't worry, I'll get it." I was absolutely mesmerized by the patience and persistence he showed in his desire to get the scene perfect.

It was very late in the day, after many takes, that the director and Mr. Cagney were finally satisfied with the scene. And we all applauded Mr. Cagney for his strong and resolute determination to get the scene right. Concentration took on a new meaning for me that day. There was something very personal and visceral in his desire. And I learned a basic lesson about filmmaking: *You do it until you get it right.*

4

IMAGINATION

Without imagination, there can be no creativeness.[1]

Constantin Stanislavski

Ninety percent of what you see and use on the stage comes from imagination.[2]

Stella Adler

You cannot say a word until you see the image and know your attitude towards it. Otherwise, your words will only be dead sounds. An Actor must see vivid images, and make his partners see them; then the audience will see them too.[3]

Sonia Moore

I've heard the expression *acting begins with a leap of the imagination*. That may be true, but sometimes it doesn't necessarily leap – sometimes it may crawl, or it may appear in unlikely places, like a pearl just waiting to be discovered. Here are two instances in which I discovered my pearls in unusual places.

Years ago, there was a television program called *Playhouse 90*. It was a program that dramatized real stories of real people. In the program entitled "Seven against the Wall" – the story of the infamous St. Valentine's Day Massacre – I played a real person, Albert Weinshank, who was the bookkeeper for the Mob. In those days, you were given a handout describing your character. One sentence caught my eye: "He was afraid of guns." When, as Albert, I was told to carry a gun by the boss, and use it if necessary, I was very nervous. I handled the gun very, very carefully. Suddenly, images began to appear. I was afraid for my family, my children. I began to re-examine my entire life and my job with these criminals. Holding that gun gave me, the actor, the *images* and the *fear* and *uncertainty* which became the nucleus for my character.

Another time, I was cast as Vittorio Mussolini, the son of Benito Mussolini, the twentieth-century Italian dictator. When Italy attacked Ethiopia, Vittorio became a hero. He was a pilot and he loved flying airplanes. It was rumored he actually said, "I still remember the effect I produced on a small group of Galla tribesmen massed around a man in black clothes. I dropped an aerial torpedo right in the middle, and the group opened up like a rose. It was most entertaining."[4] That wild image was all I needed. It gave me this character's insane joy and reckless abandon.

A prop, a statement, a piece of music, a sound, a picture, a word, a cartoon, any number of things can trigger your imagination. So always look for your pearls.

When we first begin acting, we learn the words only. We soon learn that the word is only a suggestion of what's really going on. In a play, the author is unable to put in the thoughts, dreams, inner life, or subtext of his characters. What the character sees, thinks, feels, is not written. You must imagine them.

Every character is full of images. Your job as an actor is to find the proper images that correspond to the character you are portraying. Everyone you have ever met and everything you have experienced will provide you with images.

In real life, we see real things, we hear real things, we touch real things, we smell real things, we taste real things. We live our lives with a degree of sensory involvement. But on the stage, or in front of the camera, these things are imagined by us. When the director calls "action" or when the curtain in the theatre goes up, you are meant to look out of a window and see a huge fire. There may be no fire, only a stage manager or a few actors waiting for their entrances, but you must see a fire. And that fire you see must be so real that people sitting in the audience watching you can forget all their real problems in the presence of your imaginary fire.

Imagination exercises

- You take your blind brother to the top of the Empire State Building. It is his birthday. He wants to visualize all of the sights of New York City. Describe them to him.
- Your best friend has been wrongly accused of committing murder. He is sentenced to die in the gas chamber tonight at midnight. You're asked to speak to the governor for a last-minute reprieve. It is now 11 p.m. You are speaking to a closed-circuit television camera. No one else is in the room. The governor is miles away, listening to you from his office. He can see you, but you cannot see him. Your task is to persuade the governor to order a reprieve for your friend.
- You are standing where you can see Niagara Falls or Times Square or Istanbul or the Hollywood Hills, etc. Call your wife or husband or your special friend and describe the sights to them. They could not come there with you, but you promised to call them and share the experience.
- With your imagination:

  + See a beautiful, soothing picture on the wall. Describe it.
  + See a terrifying picture on the wall. Describe it.
  + Listen to a train whistle crossing from one side of the town to the other.
  + Imagine you are listening to a 100-piece symphony orchestra.
  + Smell the salty, cool breeze of the ocean. Smell steamed clams, burning wood, hot pastrami.
  + Taste vinegar, cool lemon ice.

- Begin talking about John Smith, an imaginary person. Try to make him real. Include other people in the discussion. Question them about John Smith. Describe Smith, his habits, his clothes, his peculiar traits, and eccentricities. Defend him, accuse him, praise him. See him in your mind's eye and react to what you see.

5

BENEATH THE WORDS

Acting means dreaming at fixed moments in fixed places. (Imagination might be called dreaming.) The actor must dream his own dreams underneath the playwright's dialogue. What you see and hear on the stage is not all that the playwright has written. Beneath his words lie the dreams of the actor. If you even say a simple line, "Hello, my Darling," without a dream behind it, without a personal fantasy of some sort, you are not acting.[1]

Sir Ralph Richardson

Subtext

We speak in order to change things. We expect something to happen as a result of what we say and how we say it.

It's been said that "people go to the theatre to hear the subtext – they can always read the text at home." Beneath the text, there is the true meaning: the subtext. This subtext is not what you say, but what you mean.

For example, Masha in Anton Chekhov's *The Seagull* says, "My foot's gone to sleep" as she leaves a room. What does she really mean? We know she is in love with Treplev and is unhappily involved with Medvedenko. Among the possible meanings are:

- I have to get out of here.
- I need a drink.
- Older people bore me.
- I want to be alone.

She may speak the line, but what is really happening is beneath the line, the subtext, and that is what the audience will hear and relate to. And that is what the actor must understand. To quote my wonderful friend, the extraordinary teacher Jeff Corey, "A good improvisation should be all subtext, and no mention of text. When you perform, it's the opposite, it's all text, but the subtext makes it work."[2]

So therefore, as you approach the scene and face your fellow actors, remember, it is not what you say, it is what you mean to convey. And that is called subtext.

Inner monologue

The subtext is what you mean beneath the words when you are speaking. But what happens when you must listen to another person and you are still angry or agreeable or unsure and have not finished what you wanted to say? You literally speak to yourself. This thinking while another person is speaking is called the inner monologue. We've all done it, in our mind we continue thinking; we continue to express our thoughts, even when we are silent. These thoughts and this continuous thinking helps you come to your next moment with a clear action or decision.

Playwrights seldom describe the thoughts of their characters so the actor must create an inner monologue, just like in real life where you think, feel, and express your innermost feelings while the other character is speaking or during pauses in your own speech.

The inner monologue keeps you vital in the moment and, most importantly, makes it possible for you to attack your next moment fully, and motivated. When it is time for your line, the inner monologue will make it resonant and real.

6

SENSORY EXERCISES

The foundation of acting is the reality of doing.[1]

Sanford Meisner

There are two types of sensory exercises:

- the one-action problem
- relating to objects.

Both of these develop a heightened sense of awareness through the five senses.

The one-action problem

At the Neighborhood Playhouse School of the Theatre, which offered a very concentrated two-year program for the actor, we spent the first six months practising one-action problems. I distinctly remember such diverse actions as to draw a picture, to drink a liquid, to crawl across a room, to disguise myself, to find money. These exercises all served to sharpen the senses.

The one-action problem is a miniature scene without words. It is at the very heart of our technique as actors. It involves a simple task to be performed simply, clearly, specifically, in an urgent imaginary situation.

Within this imaginary situation, all the actor's senses are heightened. Whatever the actor beholds, touches, tastes, smells, or hears, becomes a matter of the greatest importance because the actor must stay aware to stay alive.

The formula for setting up the one-action problem

1   Start with an activity in relation to an object. It could be to:

- hide a wallet
- remove a belt
- wipe off stains
- measure a room
- erase something
- replace a key
- crawl across a room
- plant evidence
- untie a shoe
- find a letter
- copy a note
- move furniture.

2   Once you have established the activity and object, you must answer four questions:

- What do you want?
- Why do you want it?
- Where is it?
- When is it?

3   Next, to create a sense of danger or difficulty, you must provide a human obstacle, someone who opposes you within the situation: a guard, an enemy, a stern authority, a person sleeping, etc. You should also establish a time limit on accomplishing your action, since urgency is also an essential element in a successful one-action problem.

The important thing is that everything is specific to you. It isn't necessary to complete the action. What is important is what you do and what is happening to you as you attempt it.

In *On the Art of Poetry*, Aristotle wrote,

> Happiness and misery are not states of being, but forms of
> activity. The end for which we live is some form of activity ...
> Men are better or worse according to their moral bent, but they
> become happy or miserable in their actual deeds ... the revelation
> of character is subsidiary to what is done.[2]

It is almost as if Aristotle is saying you become what you do. Not
what you think or feel or hope or say, but what you do. Thus the one-
action problem teaches you *to do*. It is a miniature play that focuses on
your task. It is the beginning of your actor's technique.

A note on the one-action problem

I began my teaching career quite by accident. After World War
II, I had the GI Bill and so I returned to Staley College of the
Spoken Word in Brookline, Massachusetts. I was slightly older
than the new students and Dr. Staley asked me to assist him in the
classes. The following year, he offered me a job teaching a class on
Monday evenings. It was called Psycho-Gymnastics. The students
were older, professional men and women: lawyers, doctors, politicians, priests, rabbis, and ministers.

The idea behind the class was that every movement must be
justified. Every physical action must have a purpose behind it. I
had the students bring in a speech, poem, or a monologue from
a play. I tried to give them expressive gestures to heighten the
action. At first, some of them were a little embarrassed about the
exercise, but, after a while, they loved it and it became an evening
of learning and fun. It was, to put it simply, very exciting for me, 22
years old at the time, to be teaching all these successful people. In
my class was a tall, thin war hero who was running for Congress.
His name was John F. Kennedy.

Years later, when I was in New York and began studying the
works of Stanislavski and Sonia Moore and others, I was astounded
to discover that they called this exercise *psycho physical*. The
physical movement or action must have a clear psychological

justification. I suddenly realized that I had been teaching a form of this exercise many years earlier.

So therefore, in my classes, I always include the one-action problem. It exemplifies the idea that every action must have a purpose behind it, and it illuminates Sandy Meisner's dictum, "the foundation of acting is the reality of doing."

Relating to objects

You must learn to relate fully to familiar things as if you are seeing them and using them for the first time.

One way is to give yourself over to the observation of everyday physical activities, things we do each day. We have become almost indifferent to drinking coffee or tea, shaving, putting on makeup, eating food, etc. These activities consume a great portion of our lives, so, as actors we can learn much from these activities, if we observe them fully.

1   As you perform the following daily activities, observe with all your senses what is happening. Really see, taste, touch, smell, hear as you:

   + drink coffee or tea
   + put on your makeup
   + eat sharp cheese
   + put on your shoes
   + peel and eat an orange
   + take a cold shower
   + brush your teeth
   + shell peas
   + eat corn on the cob
   + listen to a departing car
   + arrange a vase of flowers.

2   After doing these simple activities several times with the real objects, put the object away and try to recreate through your senses the whole experience.

Taste the liquid coffee as it touches your lips and moves into your mouth and slowly passes into your throat and into your stomach. Try to get honest responses from these imagined objects.

Observe the way your hand moves as you pick up the knife to cut the cheese. Observe as you put the cheese to your nose and smell it. Don't suggest smelling it; really smell it – don't *show* us anything. You are trying to recreate something for yourself. Now, slowly, put a small piece of that cheese into your mouth. Chew it: feel the saliva in your mouth mixing with the cheese. Feel it as it passes into your throat and downward. Taste: enjoy that pungent and unique flavor. The smell remains on your hands. Enjoy.

3   After working on individual objects for a while, try combining several objects in a sensory experience. For example:

+ listen to jazz music while drinking coffee
+ put on your shoes, suddenly feel a cold draft
+ shave while smoking a cigar
+ put on your makeup while reading a magazine
+ eat sharp cheese while adding complicated figures
+ comb your hair, smell a skunk
+ read a happy letter, see a fire
+ crack walnuts, listen to the rain
+ take off damp socks, taste hot cocoa
+ put iodine on a cut, see an automobile accident.

This is relating to objects, which teaches you to observe and helps you to sharpen and heighten your five senses.

7

IMPROVISATION

If you speak any lines or do anything mechanically without fully real-
izing who you are, where you come from, why, what you want, where
you are going, and what you will do when you get there, you will be
acting without imagination.[1]

Constantin Stanislavski

A dictionary might define the word *improvise* as "to fabricate out of
what is conveniently at hand." And, in a strange way, that is what
we do when we start to improvise various situations, using our own
words and ideas to fulfill an objective.

For example, a simple situation could be if John tries to persuade
his friend Larry to loan him five hundred dollars. John must think
of all the reasons he needs the money and Larry will have his reasons
for not giving him the money. Each person must invent reasons.
You must really listen and relate to what is happening because there
is no script, no plot, only two guys who want something. And each
actor should have a *so therefore* that can drive the scene and give
them the energy to invent and use all of their resources to accom-
plish their task.

The improvisation is one of the best means of overcoming those
two bad tendencies: the need to talk, and the lack of concentration.
You act out the situation, not words from a play. You must listen and
relate to what you hear because you don't know what might be said or
done. In a play, we know what is about to happen and too many times,
we anticipate the results.

There are a variety of improvisations. They can be used:

- to create a life before a scene
- to establish a specific relationship
- to clarify events only spoken of in the script
- to open up an emotional area for the actor
- to activate the subtext: to find out what really is happening beneath the line.

Remember, since all improvisation is discovery, it's important that you don't know what the other actor will do. Also, you should listen with the same energy that you use when you are speaking.

Two-person improvisations

Take any good play, pick out an interesting two-character scene and extract the acting elements. Ask yourself: *What do I want here? Why? Where is this happening? When?* and, *What must I do to achieve my objective?*

Then improvise the situation using your own words and pursuing your objective. And don't forget your *so therefore*. As in all improvisations, you must listen and deal with a partner. Your partner will also have actions to play. To quote Sandy Meisner again, "Acting is reacting truthfully in an imaginary situation."[2] It is also trying to effect change in your partner, and dealing with whatever your partner brings to the scene.

A note on reacting truthfully

Years ago, I was playing a role on the *United States Steel Hour* television show. The star of the show was that wonderful Irish actor, Barry Fitzgerald. He was playing an old longshoreman and I was a rookie. We both sat at the bar and the action was to drink some whiskey, say a few lines, and then walk to the ship. In rehearsal, Mr. Fitzgerald took a large swig of the drink, rubbed the back of his hand across his mouth, and then looked at me and asked, "How do you like that whiskey, boy?" My line was, "It's pretty good." In rehearsal, I just drank the whiskey, said my line,

Figure 1 Barry Fitzgerald (sitting, with hat) gives Al (far right) a basic acting lesson.

and got ready to walk to the ship. Just before we were about to film the scene, Mr. Fitzgerald whispered to me, "Listen, boy, take your time, really taste that whiskey, enjoy the flavor, think about it for a while, then say your line. That way," he said, with a twinkle in his eye, "you'll get more time on camera."[3] So, on his advice, after his line, I took a nice long swig from my glass, then I slowly wiped my mouth, while I was relishing the taste, and finally I said my line. Mr. Fitzgerald smiled and shook my hand.

At the Neighborhood Playhouse I had heard Sandy Meisner say, "Acting is reacting truthfully in an imaginary situation." Now I really understood what he was talking about.

Group improvisation

If you are working with a group, here are some interesting situations you might enjoy exploring. All of these situations, incidentally, were taken from actual life experiences.

- A friend is giving a birthday party. Let us say he is a Broadway director or film producer. Several people come. Each person has a specific attitude towards the party. Each person knows: (a) what they want; (b) why they want it; (c) where they are, and; (d) when it is happening. They also should know where they have come from and the given circumstances. Perhaps among the people invited are a fellow director, an actor looking for work, a politician who uses the occasion to win votes, a young couple who announce their engagement, a pickpocket, an entertainer, etc. Given this general situation, you have to make a specific adjustment to the party, the person giving the party, and the other guests. You should know why you were invited. Within that framework, you have the impulse *to do something* at this party. If you relate to what happens, if you really listen to what is said, the scene could go any number of ways.

- You live in a boarding house. The landlord calls a meeting of all the tenants. She announces there is to be a raise in the rent and all the tenants must sign a paper agreeing to it. The boarders have different personalities with different attitudes about this problem and ask questions, make suggestions, and try to solve the problem. Among the tenants are a young lawyer, a recently arrived immigrant who can barely speak English, a bigot, a religious philosopher, a student with little money, and the landlord's lover.

- You are all actors in a touring company stranded in Hastings, Nebraska. It is winter. It is very cold. You are in the middle of a tour of a new play. The company manager calls a meeting in the dressing room after the show. He wants to continue touring the show. He can get more bookings. However, he must ask the company to work for no salary for two months until he can get the show back on its feet financially. He wants all the actors to sign an agreement to this effect. All the actors feel differently about the situation. Among the company is the star, the understudy who resents the star, a classically trained actor who believes the company should do Shakespeare, an actor with a terrible toothache, an actor with some law experience, an ingénue who has a hot date waiting outside, and a young bit player who believes in "the method".

The important thing is that you know what you want in the situation and what you'll do. This gives you the impulse to act.

8

ANIMAL STUDIES

Here, in my case, all the animals that were ever caught in traps came to my aid – a favorite instance of this is the ermine that is trapped by salt scattered upon the hard snow. This the ermine starts to lick, but the cunning mixture holds fast to its tongue, keeping it prisoner though it tries to tear itself free. Trading upon this animal torment helped me to produce a horrifying enough noise.[1]

Laurence Olivier referring to his use of animal images to produce the agonizing cry in his production of *Oedipus Rex*

1   Select an animal. It could be a cat, monkey, elephant, snake, lion, tiger, bear, dog, giraffe, peacock, hyena, gorilla, duck, chipmunk, rabbit, bull, pig, chicken, seagull, fox, crab, mouse, ostrich, goose, vulture, or any number of animals.

2   Study the animal. If you can go to a zoo, fine. If not, you must research in other ways: the movies, a special film, research books, paintings, explorations, your own backyard, YouTube, etc.

3   Bring your animal to the class and *be it for them*. That is, try to capture the flavor of the chosen animal and present your study to the class. You must walk like it, grunt or growl, and utter sounds like the animal. Include special elements that give this animal its uniqueness.

4   Pick a subject and talk to the class, using elements of the animal as you talk, for example, the way it holds its head, the way it sniffs in the air, the way it listens and reacts, the way it swiftly shifts its head or reaches with its paws. Talk from the animal's point of view.

5   Do an improvisation as a person characterized as your animal.
6   Finally, do an entire scene from a play, including outstanding elements that you have found from your animal. It isn't important to capture the whole animal. One or two elements will give the flavor and uniqueness that you desire.

Animal study exercises

Here are some suggestions for scenes to play as animals.

- A tired bear comes home to confront a tiger (for example, in *Waiting for Lefty* by Clifford Odets, the scene that begins, "Where's all the furniture, honey?").
- A frightened kitten is confronted by a peacock (for example, in *The Rainmaker* by N. Richard Nash, the characters of Starbuck and Lizzie).
- A snake talks to a tired dog (for example, in *Golden Boy* by Clifford Odets, the characters Fuseli and Lorna Moon).
- A trainer confronts a wild stallion (for example, in *The Rose Tattoo* by Tennessee Williams, the characters of Father De Leo and Serafina).
- A chipmunk meets a fox.
- An improvisation in a jail with a lion, a gorilla, a mouse, and a chicken.
- A bear meets a peacock.
- A lion in a cage meets a monkey.

The combinations are endless. The animal adds an element of creativity to the actor. It forces him or her to look outside, into the study of the world around them. The study of animals can enrich your technique, keeping it real and truthful because it is observed from life.

9

LIFE STUDIES

Nose on, wig on, makeup complete. There, staring back at me from the mirror, was my Richard, exactly as I wanted him. I'd based the makeup on the American theater director Jed Harris, the most loathsome man I'd ever met. My revenge on Jed Harris was complete.[1]

Laurence Olivier on his life image in creating the title role in *Richard III*

Using the same process as in the animal exercises, study unusual human beings with character elements you can bring to class. David Garrick, an outstanding English actor in the eighteenth century, studied a man who had gone mad after the loss of his child. He observed him daily: his manner, his peculiarities. He watched his movements, his eyes, studied his walk, listened to his speech, his child-like mumblings. When he performed *King Lear* he had taken from nature. He is reported to have said, "There it was that I learned to imitate madness; I copied nature, and to that I owed my success in King Lear."[2]

Charlie Chaplin admits his character of the Little Tramp was taken from a life study. In describing his method of work, he wrote:

> There is no study in the art of acting that requires such an accu-rate and sympathetic knowledge of human nature, as comedy work. To be successful in it, one must acquire the gift of studying men at their daily work. I find my characters in real life.[3]

John Barrymore in many of his characterizations, Marlon Brando in *On the Waterfront*, Paul Newman in *Somebody Up There Likes Me*, and, more recently, Helen Mirren, for her performance as Queen Elizabeth in the movie *The Queen*, and Jamie Foxx, for his performance as Ray Charles in the movie *Ray*, credit each convincing portrayal to the study, observation, and capturing of a real human being.

A note on a life study

My own experience with this exercise came during my student days at the Neighborhood Playhouse School of the Theatre.

I went to the Bowery in search of a real human being. I found my life study lying in the gutter in front of a cheap flophouse. He was practically dead. I remember the way he stared into space, an emptiness about him. He asked for a cigarette and when I produced a whole one, he practically devoured it, wetting it with his lips and inhaling the fumes like they were food or oxygen.

I offered to feed him: he reluctantly accepted. He wanted a drink. We sat opposite one another as he slowly ate beef stew in a greasy restaurant, underneath the Third Avenue El. He chewed his food very slowly: his teeth had decayed. He spoke softly, almost like a woman. He left after the meal, having asked for more cigarettes. He had smoked the first one I had given him down to the very end. He had a genius for manipulating the butt around the sides of his mouth so it didn't burn him. He was an artist in the way he could move that cigarette around.

I was able to capture his use of the cigarette for a characterization in class. I also used the slow, methodical manner of his eating his food: chewing it slowly, as if it hurt; soaking bread into the stew; staring into space, vacant, not questioning, an empty shell living in some distant past. The food was almost punishment for him, like a schoolboy required to eat spinach before dessert. The cigarette was dessert. The cigarette was a glorious adventure.

The world is full of human beings who are the subjects for our study. They can provide great incentive for honest characterization. The process is the same as in animal studies.

1   Study the character.
2   Present your study to the class.
3   Don't talk about it, do it.
4   Talk to the class on any subject using the elements from your life study.
5   Do an improvisation using elements from the character you have studied.
6   Finally, select a scene. Play a character using one or two elements from your life study.

Naturally, whatever you do must become a natural part of the character you are playing. You must justify the behavior that you bring from your life study. The reason the man smoked the cigarette butt to the very end was he didn't know when he would get another one. His attitude was as if this were his last cigarette ever. So he consumed it like oxygen. The reason he chewed his food so slowly was it probably hurt him to chew. His gums were probably sore. His teeth hurt. It was as if he had to eat corn on the cob with his first set of dentures, apprehensively and very, very carefully.

So, actors, carry your pad and pencil, keep sharp eyes and acute senses. The world is your classroom. People are your material. Wherever you go – no matter the time of day, no matter the situation, no matter the personal involvement or your mental, physical, or spiritual disposition – there might be the seed of a great character just waiting for you out there. The practise of life studies is continual.

Here are some examples of life studies that have helped me to create characters.

When I played Arthur Goldman in *The Man in the Glass Booth* by Robert Shaw, my director Robert G. Egan and I visited the Holocaust Museum in Los Angeles. We studied film of Adolf Eichmann and the Nazis. We observed their behavior and their attitude. We heard their justifications. Goldman was a Jew who had lost his wife and children in the concentration camps. He is now a successful businessman, on the verge of a nervous breakdown. He assumes the character of a Nazi, praises Adolf Hitler, wears the Nazi uniform, and struts around his office. Only near the end, when an old lady recognizes him from the concentration camp, does he literally and emotionally collapse and enter the glass booth, naked, and ashamed.

Figure 2 Al in *The Man in the Glass Booth* as Arthur Goldman, a Jew suffering from terrible guilt and on the verge a mental breakdown, donning a Nazi uniform and praising Adolf Hitler. (Photo credit: © Eric E. Emerson, Tanstaafl Photography.)

One summer, I was offered the role of Sitting Bull in a wonderful play called *Indians* by Arthur Kopit. As part of my research, I went to the town of Tama, Iowa, where they were having a Native American celebration or *chautauqua*. As I approached the front entrance of this huge circus tent, I saw that it was very crowded. So I went around the back and managed to crawl underneath the tent where I could observe the Native Americans getting ready for their show. One Native American caught my attention. He was sitting at a table, looking forlorn. As I crept closer, I could see that he was alone; part of his costume was on the table. He was looking off into the distance and he was biting his fingernails. He seemed very worried. Then they announced that his group was next on the program. He rose from the table, put on the rest of his costume, including a rich and colorful headdress, and began preparing for his entrance. He began chanting like a happy warrior. I sensed he was really embarrassed about what he had to do. And then I thought about the great Native American chief, Sitting Bull. He had to perform in Buffalo Bill's Wild West show. He, too, was ashamed for what he had to do to earn money so he could buy food and supplies for his people. He, too, had to live a lie. This knowledge became the foundation for my work and study of the character.

Figure 3 Sitting Bull) in ceremonial attire. National Museum of the American Indian, Smithsonian Institution. (Photo by William Notman and Son Co.)

Mr. Harris was the hardware store owner in *The Wonder Years* on television. He was a man living in the past: strict, dedicated to his way of life, unable to move into the present or see the future. My father, Antonio, was my model. He spent many years in veterans' hospitals as a result of wounds suffered fighting in World War I. When he periodically returned home he couldn't seem to adjust or accept the pace of life. The routine in the hospital had become his way of life. He disliked telephones and radios and television. They were too noisy and upset his routine. He could not deal with them. And yet he was a good man. He tried to catch up, but so many things had changed that he preferred to keep his own quiet, peaceful ways.

Sal Giordano was the grandfather in *Life Goes On*, also on television. A gregarious man, he enjoyed a glass of wine and listening to opera. He would laugh and sing at the drop of a hat. My own grandfather, Stefano Coletti, was my model. He was the happiest man I

Figure 4 My father Antonio, relaxing in the peaceful environment of the veterans' hospital in Rutland, MA.

ever knew. He and his wife had ten children. They never owned a car. They rarely took trips. He could sing out loud. And, on special occasions, they would make a dish called polenta, made with cornmeal. They added tomato sauce and stretched out the polenta across a table. Then we would all sit around the table and, on a signal, would eat

Figure 5 My grandfather Stefano Coletti who taught me how to enjoy a glass of wine and how to laugh, and to never give up on my hopes and dreams.

our portion of the polenta pie until someone could devour their share and get to the middle of the pie where a penny or a nickel awaited the winner. And we all laughed and played music for the rest of the day.

On the west side of Manhattan, during a slow period, I took a job working on the docks for the Pennsylvania Railroad. It was reminiscent of the movie *On the Waterfront*. We lugged huge boxes and crates onto platforms, then into railroad cars and ferries heading for New Jersey. I was able to study the work routine, the comradeship, and physicality of the men. I saw the violence and heard the rough language. Years later I got to play Eddie Carbone in *A View from the Bridge* by Arthur Miller. I tried to picture Eddie working on the docks. He was a good man but I could not picture him laughing and dealing with the other men. I sensed that he was basically a quiet man who truly came alive at home in front of his two women: Beatrice his wife, and Catherine his niece. Here, he could laugh, tell stories, and

Figure 6 Al as Eddie Carbone in *A View from the Bridge* with Muriel Dusel as Beatrice.

be the king. To me, this was the heart of this character. At the climax of the play, when his life at home is threatened, he falls apart and calls the immigration people, actions that eventually bring about his own death. Working on the docks for the Pennsylvania Railroad gave me the life study for Eddie Carbone.

10

EMOTIONAL RECALL

The basic problem in acting is to learn to be private in public.[1]

Constantin Stanislavski

Sometimes, a scene presents an emotional block for the actor. The emotion is not free, the acting is tense. All the actions seem correct, but the emotional undercurrent is bottled up. At these times, it may be useful to explore emotional exercises.

The process of emotional recall is sensory. That is, you don't go looking for the emotion directly. You describe the event through your five senses, in the first person, as though it is happening now. You remember certain experiences which once moved you, which stimulated an emotion in you, which had deep meaning for you at the time.

This experience can be a happy one. It can be a sad one. It can be a complex experience that produced mixed emotions – perhaps one where you had to do something that went against your nature, for example, you had to leave, but you didn't want to go.

Experiences, particularly of childhood, can be recalled in the same manner. Like a reporter, use the five senses to describe the event. The colors, the sizes, the smells, the tastes, the feel of the material, the sounds. Be specific. In the first person describe it as if it were happening now.

As you see the people you know, hear their voices, touch them, smell the fresh air, taste the food, remember what you did at that time; the emotion of that experience will return. It may take a while, but soon a phrase or a sound or an object will bring back that honest emotion you once experienced.

It is useful to begin with an object, a phrase, a sound, or an experience. Sometimes a bicycle or a doll or a pair of shoes will set the actor into recalling a significant experience of his or her life. No matter how you begin or what element you use to start the exercise, the process is the same.

One of my students began with the object *scissors*. This student, Stephen, recalled his uncle Tony. Tony was a barber and every Saturday morning Tony gave the boy Stephen a free haircut. Stephen recalled the way Tony flourished his scissors in the air with the manner of an artist as he sat in the barber's chair. Stephen always associated the scissors and the haircut with his uncle Tony. He could see scissors or think of them in an emotional recall exercise and it brought up all kinds of stimuli associated with his uncle Tony.

Sometimes a phrase works as well. The day Stephen's uncle Tony died was a Saturday and the boy, not knowing, went to the barbershop as usual for his free haircut. A schoolmate, seeing him standing in front of the closed barbershop yelled, "Hey, Stephano, your Uncle Tony's dead, eh? Well, no more free haircuts!"

That phrase – "No more free haircuts!" – can begin an emotional experience for this student which can release a deep well of honest feeling for use in a scene or a play or an exercise.

A note on emotional memory

A sound can bring back an emotion. When my own father died, I was performing in a summer theatre in Pennsylvania. I took the first train back home. My senses were very acute. I began to think about my father, his life, our relationship, how we never really were able to get to know each other. I had been away at school all winter and now this summer job prevented me from spending time at home, so I felt guilty and mad at myself, all at the same time.

The train moving on the tracks made a *clakety-clack-clackety-clack-clackety-clack* sound. It sounded very loud, persistent, and ominous. It had a steady, pulsating rhythm that played in my head long afterward.

To this day, whenever I hear or recall those train noises – *clackety-clack-clackety-clack-clackety-clack* – as the train rolled on through Pennsylvania, through New York and Connecticut to Massachusetts, I always think about my father. I always experience that guilt.

So therefore, a word of caution. In the 1930s and 1940s the actors in The Group Theatre in New York were experimenting with emotional memory. Stella Adler then went to Paris and worked with Stanislavski for over a month. Sandy Meisner, one of the original members of The Group, remembers, "What Stella told us was that Stanislavski recommended using the 'given circumstances of the play' or the 'background of the situation in the play' or the magical *as if* to induce emotion. And, that 'emotional memory is to be used only when nothing else works.'"[2]

To this day there is considerable debate on the use of emotional memory in acting, and I recommend using it only with caution, particularly for beginning actors.

Part 2

SCENE WORK

II

CHARACTER ANALYSIS

First of all, read the entire play or the script. Try to discover the main idea behind the story. What is the main conflict? Read it again. Try to find your point of personal identification. See yourself in the midst of the circumstances of this story. What special appeal is there about this character? What unique problems do you see? *What must you do to yourself in order to cross into the life of this imaginary character?*

Now, make an analysis of the character.

Actors have different approaches to character analysis. Some prefer writing a biography exploring the character's inner life, his or her childhood, family, education, relationships, and lifestyle.

Others prefer to go to the actual location where their character might live so they can get a sense of the neighborhood. They study the people they see, ask questions, and try to imagine their character living there. Al Pacino, when he played Frank Serpico in *Serpico*, hung around the police station. He got to know Serpico very well and he studied him. He even went on police calls to get an emotional feel of what these men actually went through.

Anthony Quinn once spoke about how he worked on his characters. He would make two columns. One was headed "Anthony Quinn" and the other would be headed by the name of the character he was about to play. Then he would compare the traits of the imaginary character against his own traits. Where there were differences, Mr. Quinn would work on those elements until he could make them his own. For example, if the imaginary character was a college professor and taught the plays of Shakespeare, Mr. Quinn would study Shakespeare until he was comfortable in that area.

In any case, however you approach the analysis, you should make a strong attempt to get under the skin of the people you are to portray, to transform their imaginary life into your own reality. An analysis of your own character definitely helps, as well.

Once you have completed the character analysis, you should explore:

- the spine of the play
- the spine of your character
- your objective in the scene
- your actions in the scene
- the *as if*
- preparation
- scenes.

12

THE SPINE OF THE PLAY

The term *spine of the play* was popularized by Harold Clurman, co-founder and managing director of the famous Group Theatre which flourished in New York City from 1931 to 1941. (In addition, Clurman was the director of the original productions of *Awake and Sing*, *Golden Boy*, *Rocket to the Moon*, and *Member of the Wedding*, and author of *The Fervent Years*, the story of the Group Theatre.) He describes the spine this way:

> What is the basic action of the play? What is the play about from the standpoint of the character's principal conflict? What fundamental desire does the plot of his play symbolize, what deep struggle gives it shape and direction? What is the play's core?[1]

Every play has a spine. Clurman talks of the spine of Clifford Odets's play *Night Music* as "a search for a home."[2] For Gordon Craig, the great designer, the spine of the play *Hamlet* is "a search for truth."[3] For Robert Lewis, the spine of William Saroyan's play *My Heart's in the Highlands* is people "eager to give things to one another."[4]

Richard Boleslavsky, a disciple of Stanislavski and a brilliant teacher in his own right, compares the spine of the play to the trunk of a tree.

> Look at that tree. It is the protagonist of all arts; it is an ideal structure of action. Upward movement and sideways resistance, balance and growth ... look at the trunk – straight, proportioned, harmonious with the rest of the tree, supporting every part of it. It is the leading strain, "leitmotif" in music, a director's idea of

action in a play; the architect's foundation; the poet's thought in a sonnet.[5]

So, the spine of the play, the main idea behind the play – the active desire which propels the play forward – must be stated. This is your first task.

13

THE SPINE OF THE CHARACTER

Once you have the spine of the play, you must discover the spine of your character. What overwhelming desire compels your character throughout the play and motivates your behavior from start to finish? What do you want? What is your life goal? What is your psychological and spiritual drive and desire? What is the spine of your character? How does this relate to the spine of the play?

The director of *A Streetcar Named Desire*, Elia Kazan, discussed the spines of the major characters in that play:

- to find protection – the spine for Blanche
- to hold onto Stanley – the spine for Stella
- to keep things his way – the spine for Stanley
- to get away from his mother – the spine for Mitch.[1]

Your character can want to seek revenge, to gain freedom, to find love, to get security, to own money, to keep privacy, to enjoy sex, to satisfy cravings, to convert the world, to destroy the world, to improve life, to find happiness, to find the right answers, to grab some joy, etc.

Whatever it is, your character's spine must be clear and specific. It must also relate to the spine of the play. If the spine of the play is a *search for truth*, how does the spine of your character affect that search? Does it help it along? Does it retard it? Does it detract from it? Do you work with the spine or do you oppose it?

For example, in the play *A View from the Bridge* by Arthur Miller, a Brooklyn longshoreman named Eddie Carbone lives with his wife Beatrice and his niece, Catherine. They are comparatively happy.

These two women serve him, listen to his stories, enjoy him. But now the niece wants to take a job and become independent. Eddie has developed an extremely possessive attachment to her. He is overly concerned about protecting her. When she falls in love with a young immigrant, Eddie is determined to stop it and to destroy this young man. Eddie wants *to keep things the same* and prevent his little girl from ever growing up and leaving him. That is his spine.

14

YOUR OBJECTIVE IN THE SCENE

Now you have the spine of the play and the spine of your character. The scene lies before you. Read it, study it. What happens in it? What do you want in this scene? Why are you there? The answers, of course, should relate to the spine of the play and the spine of your character. This thing you want in the scene is called your objective.

Let's analyze a scene from *A View from the Bridge*. This play is fashioned after a true story. The lead character, Eddie, breaks the code of his neighborhood, calls the immigration department and squeals on some illegal immigrants and, therefore, must die.

The scene we'll look at occurs several weeks after the immigrants arrive and are sharing the house with Eddie and his family. One of the immigrants, Rudolfo, has been dating Catherine, and Eddie has become very sullen and irritable. Here is the scene.

(*Eddie is standing at the doorway of the house. His wife, Beatrice, enters from the street. She sees Eddie, smiles at him. He looks away. She starts to enter the house when Eddie speaks.*)

EDDIE: It's after eight.

BEATRICE: Well, it's a long show at the Paramount.

EDDIE: They must've seen every picture in Brooklyn by now. He's supposed to stay in the house when he ain't working. He ain't supposed to go advertising himself.

BEATRICE: Well, that's his trouble, what do you care? If they pick him up they pick him up, that's all. Come in the house.

EDDIE: What happened to the stenography? I don't see her practice
  no more.

BEATRICE: She'll get back to it; she's excited, Eddie.

EDDIE: She tell you anything?

BEATRICE: What's the matter with you? He's a nice kid, what do you
  want from him?

EDDIE: That's a nice kid? He gives me the heeby-jeebies.

BEATRICE: Ah, go on, you're just jealous.

EDDIE: Of him? Boy, you don't think much of me.

BEATRICE: I don't understand you; what's so terrible about him?

EDDIE: You mean it's all right with you? That's gonna be her husband?

BEATRICE: Why? He's a nice fella, hard workin', he's a good-lookin'
  fella.

EDDIE: He sings on the ships, didja know that?

BEATRICE: What do you mean, he sings?

EDDIE: Just what I said, he sings. Right on the deck, all of a sudden
  – a whole song comes out of his mouth – with motions. You
  know what they're callin' him now? Paper Doll they're callin'
  him, Canary. He's like a weird. He comes out on the pier, one-
  two-three, it's a regular free show.

BEATRICE: Well, he's a kid; he don't know how to behave himself
  yet.

EDDIE: And with that whacky hair; he's like a chorus girl or sup'm.

BEATRICE: So he's blond, so …

EDDIE: I just hope that's his regular hair, that's all I hope.

BEATRICE: You crazy or sup'm?

EDDIE: What's so crazy? I don't like his whole way.

BEATRICE: Listen, you never seen a blond guy in your life? What
  about Whitey Balso?

EDDIE: Sure, but Whitey don't sing; he don't do like that on the
  ships.

BEATRICE: Well, maybe that's the way they do in Italy.

EDDIE: Then why don't his brother sing? Marco goes around like a
  man; nobody kids Marco. I tell you the truth I'm surprised I have
  to tell you all this. I mean I'm surprised, Bea.

BEATRICE: Listen, you ain't gonna start nothin' here.

EDDIE: I ain't startin' nothin', but I ain't gonna stand around lookin'
  at that. For that character I didn't bring her up. I swear, Bea, I'm

surprised at you; I sit there waitin' for you to wake up but everything is great with you.

BEATRICE: No, everything ain't great with me.

EDDIE: No?

BEATRICE: No. But I got other worries.

EDDIE: Yeah.

BEATRICE: Yeah, you want me to tell you?

EDDIE: Why? What worries you got?

BEATRICE: When am I gonna be a wife again, Eddie?

EDDIE: I ain't been feelin' good. They bother me since they came.

BEATRICE: It's almost three months, you don't feel good they're only here a couple of weeks. It's three months, Eddie.

EDDIE: I don't know, Bea – I don't want to talk about it.

BEATRICE: What's the matter, Eddie, you don't like me, heh?

EDDIE: What do you mean, I don't like you? I said I don't feel good, that's all.

BEATRICE: Well, tell me, am I doing something wrong? Talk to me.

EDDIE: I can't. I can't talk about it.

BEATRICE: Well, tell me what …

EDDIE: I got nothin' to say about it! I'll be all right, Bea; just lay off me, will ya? I'm worried about her.

BEATRICE: The girl is gonna be eighteen years old, it's time already.

EDDIE: Bea, he's taking her for a ride.

BEATRICE: All right, that's her ride. What're you gonna stand over her till she's forty? Eddie, I want you to cut it out now, you hear me? I don't like it … Now, come in the house.

EDDIE: I want to take a walk, I'll be in right away.

BEATRICE: They ain't goin' to come any quicker if you stand in the street; it's ain't nice, Eddie.

EDDIE: I'll be in right away. Go ahead. (*He walks right, she goes into the house.*)

Excerpt from "Act 1", from *A View from the Bridge* by Arthur Miller, copyright © 1955, 1957, 1960, copyright renewed © 1983, 1985, 1988 by Arthur Miller. Used by permission of Viking Penguin, a division of Penguin Group (USA) Inc., and the Wylie Agency LLC.

In this scene, Eddie's objective is *to get Beatrice on his side* – to have her agree that this boy is no good for his little girl. He feels that he is protecting Catherine. Beatrice's objective is *to assure Eddie that all is right and natural*. She suspects that he is too involved. She also feels unloved and wants her husband back.

Now, let's look at another scene in the comedy *Tchin-Tchin* by Sidney Michaels, based on the French comedy by Francois Billetdoux.

This is the opening scene of the play. Caesario Grimaldi has come to meet Pamela Pew-Pickett at the English restaurant in the Rockefeller Center. His wife and her husband are having an affair. They meet to prepare plans to break up the affair. In this scene, Caesario has as his objective to *avoid reality by getting drunk*. Pamela's objective is *to deal with reality by making plans*. He succeeds in his objective. She does not. Here's the scene.

CAESARIO: (*Enters*) Mrs. Pamela Pickett?
PAMELA: Pew-Pickett.
CAESARIO: Caesario Grimaldi at your service.
PAMELA: How do you do?
CAESARIO: How do you do? Pew?
PAMELA: Hyphen Pickett. Pew is my maiden name.
CAESARIO: Oh, you kept your maiden name?
PAMELA: Yes, England is full of Pews. Do you have the photograph?
    (*He shows her photograph*) Yes, that is he. (*She shows him photograph*)
CAESARIO: That's her.
(*WAITER enters, begins to clear table.*)
PAMELA: Be careful.
CAESARIO: Oh – allora noi parliamo Italiano?
PAMELA: I beg your pardon?
CAESARIO: Do you speak Italian?
PAMELA: Arrivederci –
CAESARIO: Como?
PAMELA: – is the only Italian I speak.
CAESARIO: Oh!
PAMELA: Est-ce que vous parlez Francais?
CAESARIO: I'm an American citizen.
PAMELA: Well, let us speak in English.
CAESARIO: That's a beautiful language.
PAMELA: And one we both speak. Won't you sit down, Mr. Grimaldi?

CAESARIO: Thank you. (*He removes hat and coat and places them on the chair*) I've been running all day in taxi-cabs. My business booms in December. I guess I'm five minutes late.

PAMELA: Seven minutes.

CAESARIO: Oh, then, I'm two minutes slow. Have you been waiting long?

PAMELA: No. No. Just seven minutes. Now, Mr. Grimaldi, as we are pressed for time –

CAESARIO: (*Snaps his fingers to Waiter who steps up to table*) May I take the liberty of offering you a little wet courage, dear lady?

PAMELA: I'm having my tea, thank you.

CAESARIO: A little hotter pot, perhaps?

PAMELA: I only drink tea when it cools.

CAESARIO: Is that right?

PAMELA: I have a mouth that is especially sensitive to extremes of temperature.

CAESARIO: Is that right?

PAMELA: That is right, Mr. Grimaldi.

CAESARIO: (*To waiter*) Uh – two double scotches – on the rocks, please. (*A look from Pamela*) That's so I won't have to disturb him four times. You know, I must say, your idea of the photographs was nothing short of brilliant. I mean, how else would we have known each other.

PAMELA: We are now the only two people in this restaurant, Mr. Grimaldi. Surely, sooner or later, it would have occurred to one of us that the other one of us was – the other one of us.

CAESARIO: That's right! Your husband, since he's a doctor, he keeps himself – fit – and in trim, I suppose?

PAMELA: Fanatically. Wheat germ. Dumbbells. Squash courts. A plate of prunes daily.

CAESARIO: (*Referring to photograph*) He's a husky, handsome young fellow.

PAMELA: That's the Doctor's favorite picture of himself. Taken twenty-five years ago.

CAESARIO: Oh. Well, as you suggested, I looked for it and I found it in my wife's lingerie drawer. There it was – right on top.

PAMELA: And I, this, of Mrs. Grimaldi, in the Doctor's copy of "Childhood Diseases."

CAESARIO: My wife is much prettier in the flesh. Here her ears stick out. Actually they lie very close to her head.

PAMELA: I'd rather not discuss anything intimate.

CAESARIO: Okay! We'll talk in broad general terms.

PAMELA: We must be bold!

CAESARIO: I can't. I'm Catholic.

PAMELA: What do you mean?

CAESARIO: Divorce is out.

PAMELA: And I am British. I'll never let Dr. Pickett go! (*The Waiter enters – places two double scotches on table and exits*)

CAESARIO: Good for you! Cheerio! (*Hits her teacup with his glass and drinks*)

Tchin-Tchin by Sidney Michaels. Copyright © 1962,
Sidney Michaels, Warner LeRoy

That's how *Tchin-Tchin* begins. Before the scene is over, Caesario will consume six double scotches and avoid discussing plans while Pamela literally has to carry him out. The people are incongruous, the lines are funny, but the actors have clear objectives to play.

15

YOUR ACTIONS IN THE SCENE

An actor becomes an actor when he masters the choice of actions.[1]
Constantin Stanislavski

Once you know what you want in the scene, your next step is to discover what you do to get what you want. These things you do are called actions.

The word "actor" means someone who does something, who behaves in a certain way – who acts. All you can act are actions. You cannot act emotions or feelings, because they are results. You cannot act words, because they are merely the indication of something going on beneath the words. In order to act, you must do something.

The thing you do is called *the action*.

You can insult your brother, persuade your friend, plead with your father, intimidate your partner, beg for money, comfort a sick friend, question your enemy, accuse somebody, complain about something, threaten someone, avoid someone, stop an argument, apologize, or greet a friend, etc.

Whatever it is, it must be clear and specific. And you should find strong verbs that get you going, for instance, not *to lecture* but *to demand action*; not *to question* but *to insist*.

Give your action a name. For instance, Kitty in *The Time of Your Life* by William Saroyan begins her famous monologue, "I dream of home. Christ, I always dream of home. I've no home. I've no place. But I always dream of all of us together again."[2] What is she doing? Is she reminiscing or complaining or giving information or trying to explain something? Find the action to play, give it a name, and that will help you find the character.

Every scene consists of a series of actions and an objective. You want something, so you do something to get it (as in life). One of the best teachers I ever studied with was Sanford Meisner. He had a favorite saying, "You cannot act on maybe. Know what you want and know it fully and specifically, then, move ahead."[3]

Let's return to the scene from *A View from the Bridge*. Here Eddie wants to get Beatrice on his side – to have her agree that this boy, Rudolfo, is no good for his little girl. Look at what he does, his *actions* in sequence.

1 He *complains* ("It's after eight.")
2 He *questions* ("What happened to the stenography?")
3 He *insults* the boy ("He gives me the heeby-jeebies.")
4 He *mocks* the boy ("He sings on the ships … ")
5 He *suggests* the boy is gay ("He's like a chorus girl or sup'm.")
6 He *praises* Marco ("Marco goes around like a man … ")
7 He *attacks* Beatrice ("I sit there waitin' for you to wake up, but everything's great with you.")
8 He *makes a weak excuse* ("I ain't been feelin' good. They bother me since they came.")
9 He *makes more excuses* ("I'm worried about her.")
10 He *gives up and walks away* ("I want to take a walk.")

Beatrice suspects that Eddie is too emotionally involved and wants to assure him that everything is right and natural. And, she wants her husband back. Look at what she does, her *actions* in sequence.

1 She *makes light* of it ("If they pick him up they pick him up, that's all.")
2 She *assures* him ("She'll get back to it … ")
3 She *teases* him ("Ah, go on, you're just jealous.")
4 She *defends* the boy ("He's a nice fella, hard workin … ")
5 She *excuses* the boy ("Well, he's a kid … ")
6 She *warns* Eddie ("Listen, you ain't gonna start nothin' here.")
7 She *complains* ("No, everything ain't great with me.")
8 She *pleads* with him ("What's the matter, Eddie, you don't like me, heh?")

9   She *spells it out* ("The girl is gonna be eighteen years old, it's time already.")
10 She *lets him have it* ("You gonna stand over her till she's forty?")

Now, let's return to the scene from *Tchin-Tchin*. Caesario wants to avoid reality by getting drunk. Look at what he does, his *actions* in sequence.

1   He *greets* Pamela ("Mrs. Pamela Pickett?")
2   He *tries to cover up* ("Oh – allora noi parliamo Italiano?")
3   He *apologizes* ("I guess I'm five minutes late.")
4   He *offers her a drink* ("May I take the liberty of offering you a little wet courage, dear lady?")
5   He *orders two double scotches* ("That's so I won't have to disturb him four times.")
6   He *flatters* her ("I must say, your idea of the photographs was nothing short of brilliant.")
7   He *comments* on the pictures ("Your husband, since he's a doctor he keeps himself – fit – and in trim, I suppose?)
8   He *explains* his position ("Okay! We'll talk in broad, general terms.")
9   He *celebrates* ("Cheerio!")

As the scene progresses, he will reminisce, tell stories, offer more drinks, tell jokes, insist Pamela drink with him, cry in his cup, sing a song, and make a pass at Pamela. All these actions not only describe the man, but they give the actor clear things to do.

Pamela, for her part, wants to deal with reality by making plans. Look at what she does, her *actions* in sequence.

1   She *greets him* ("How do you do?")
2   She *questions* him ("Do you have the photograph?")
3   She *urges secrecy* ("Be careful.")
4   She *chides him* for being late ("Seven minutes.")
5   She *refuses to drink with him* ("I'm having my tea, thank you.")
6   She *clarifies for him* ("That's the Doctor's favorite picture of himself. Taken twenty-five years ago.")
7   She *orders him* ("We must be bold!")

As the scene progresses, Pamela will also question him, refuse more drinks, try to get him to discuss the problem, explain herself, decide to leave, agree to stay, explain why she came, describe her work, restate the problem, remind him that action is required, offer to pay the check, take charge, and finally, she will reassure him.

> Your scene ... is a long string of beads – beads of action. You play with them as you play with a rosary. You can start anywhere – anytime – and go as far as you wish, if you have a good hold on the beads themselves.
>
> Richard Boleslavsky[4]

At this point, you as an actor know the spine of the play and have discovered the spine of your character. The scene rests before you. You have decided what you want in the scene – your objective. You also have studied the scene and broken it into the things you do – your actions.

Anywhere in the play, the director should be able to stop the rehearsal and ask the actor, "What are you doing?" The prepared actor should be able to answer clearly and specifically – "I am doing this."

A good actor can take any scene from any play and discover the actions within that scene. These are the gems you build on. In performance, you set your mind on what you want, and then go out and play your actions.

The actor sees actions, things to be done. The actor sees objectives, things to want. The actor sees a spine, things to believe in. This is what differentiates the actor from the layperson.

Here are some selected actions to employ when working on scenes. These are beads of action that will stir you to play the scene. As you chose them, be specific, be daring. The use of unique actions played fully leads to fascinating, captivating characters and memorable behavior. Consider these actions but also dig up your own – especially ones the character you are working on would use to get what he or she wants. Use a good source like *Roget's Thesaurus of English Words and Phrases* and find the most colorful and descriptive verbs. Write them down right in your script so when you rehearse you're thinking of what you're doing, not just what you're saying.

laugh at	bait
walk a tightrope	declare
fish for a compliment	deflate
scrutinize	demolish
open the eyes of	slam the door on
clarify	spur on
teach	throw down the gauntlet
make fun of	uplift
bury your fangs in	beg forgiveness
walk on eggs	kindle the flame with
beat a hasty retreat	stonewall
draw attention	prop up
insist	freeze-out
slam the door on	tantalize
plunge a knife into	turn your back on

16

THE *AS IF*

Once you know what you are doing in the play, you have satisfied the first step: you have made the play clear. The next step is to make the character clear.

The *what* makes the play, the *as if* makes the character.

There are many different ways of playing an action. For example, you can tell a story:

- with rich enjoyment
- with hesitation
- *as if* it were a memorized speech
- *as if* you have a violent headache
- *as if* your life depended on it
- *as if* everything you say makes you sad.

The *as if* colors your action, gives it richness and clearly places the stamp on your character, because your character would do things a special way, a unique way. Remember the character from the Bowery (in Chapter 9, Life Studies)? Remember how he smoked that cigarette? It was as if it were oxygen and he inhaled with the desperation of a man who thought this was his last cigarette.

Every character will play his or her actions the way he or she alone would do them. Of course, to comprehend the *as ifs* you must know the life of the character, the given circumstances of his or her existence. You must know what motivates him or her and what special qualities set him or her apart from other people.

The *as ifs* are how you play the action. While the action impels your character toward their objective, the *as if* enhances the basic action and gives your character individuality and verve. For example, the action *to threaten* could, used alone, lead to a generalized cliché of menace. But if you add "*as if* every syllable I utter is a bullet," or "*as if* I wish to grind you into a pulp," the character immediately takes on a unique and specific dimension.

Any action can be executed in countless ways. The countless ways are the *as ifs*. Here's a short representative list. Again, add your own, apply them to your working characters, note them down for reference, and act them out to see what works best.

As if ... everything you say makes you sad.
As if ... I am among movie stars at a premiere.
As if ... I have a vinegary taste in my mouth.
As if ... leeches are crawling all over me.
As if ... my breath smells.
As if ... I am a lion in a cage.
As if ... I am walking down a dangerous cliff.
As if ... I have two minutes left.
As if ... I have a terrible toothache.
As if ... everything I say is an important quote.
As if ... I'm talking to a dog.
As if ... I'm a top-notch district attorney.
As if ... I'm walking on hot coals.
As if ... I've just won the lottery.
As if ... I'm on my third mint julep.
As if ... I'm in quicksand.
As if ... I can't take a deep breath.
As if ... I keep walking into an ice-cold shower.
As if ... my knees have turned to jelly.
As if ... I have to scratch my big toe.
As if ... I'm talking to a drunken friend.
As if ... I'd like to slap you.
As if ... I can't stop crying.
As if ... I think you're weird.
As if ... I can't look you in the eye.
As if ... I'm entering a magnificent cathedral.

As if … I'm listening to sexy music.
As if … I'm wearing a colorful mask.
As if … I have a violent headache.
As if … I'm being questioned by an unfriendly cop.
As if … I'm hot enough to faint.
As if … my jaws are locked.
As if … I'm a clown at a circus.
As if … my voice grates on my ears.
As if … my belt is too tight.
As if … I'm seeing double.
As if … everything I say is a maybe.
As if … I can't end a sentence.
As if … you remind me of someone I can't remember.
As if … everyone is talking too fast for me.
As if … this is a dream.
As if … I'm talking to a child.
As if … I must touch everything.
As if … my pants are falling down.
As if … I've just been hit by pigeon dung.
As if … I've heard it all before.
As if … I'm including you in my holy plan.
As if … I'm a General planning the invasion of Europe.
As if … my lips hurt.
As if … I'm absolutely alone.
As if … I'd like to make you squirm.
As if … everything you say strikes me as funny.
As if … I'm fascinated by the sores on your face.
As if … your voice lulls me to sleep.
As if … the air smells suddenly rancid.

As if exercises

1   Take any action and add an *as if* to it. Create a situation and improvise. For example:

+ Ask a favor … *as if* you are a whipped dog.
+ Brag … *as if* you've just won a $10,000 jackpot.
+ Threaten … *as if* you are a crooked district attorney.

- ✦ Tell a story ... *as if* you are listening to sexy music.
- ✦ Question ... *as if* your tongue is very heavy.
- ✦ Insist on an answer ... *as if* every syllable is a bullet.
- ✦ Complain ... *as if* you can't focus your eyes.
- ✦ Give orders ... *as if* you're in an ice-cold shower.
- ✦ Sing a song ... *as if* you're a bird flying.
- ✦ Dance ... *as if* you must touch everything.

2   Try different *as ifs* using the same actions.
3   You have actions to play and *as ifs* you have chosen. Now add a personal element to this problem. This requires you to find an emotional meaning suitable to this problem. In other words, personalize the emotional content of this scene. I am reminded of a statement of Sandy Meisner: "You must grope to discover what it means to you – and then you must test, try, probe, to find a way to do it so that what it means to you comes out in your acting."[1]
4   Take any scene and extract the actions. Now add the *as ifs* and personal elements. Improvise on the given circumstances of the scene. Paul Muni's method of personalizing was putting notations on the margins of his script.

> Sometimes I change the shadings of the words because they have assumed a new significance. Now they begin to live. During this process I often note in the margin of the script, associations and parallel feelings which have come to me while I was learning my lines.[2]

How you perform the action is what stimulates your creative imagination. The *as if* is the great key that helps you fuse your talent onto the character you are creating.

A note on *As ifs*

During my long career, I've used many *as ifs*. Once, playing the head of a crime syndicate, I didn't want to yell or come on too strong, so I decided to play this boss as if I was a kind priest. This helped me to remain calm, listen, and talk softly – all of which proved most effective. On the other hand, in the movie *Romero* I played a bishop who was the military vicar. This time I was playing a real priest, but did so as if I was a waterfront boss. That choice helped me to find the power and bluntness I felt this character would use.

In improvisations and exercises, the question is, *What would I do in this situation*? But, in a play or scene or monologue, the author has already determined what you would do. So, you must find ways of justifying the behavior of this character. The question now becomes, *What must I do to myself in order to do what this character does in this situation*? You must find a way, within yourself, to make it possible to do what this imaginary character does. And you must do it in a natural and completely honest way – so that it seems the only possible way to go at that time.

A scene is a journey. Be open to all the possibilities. It happens along the way. You take a train or a bus or a car from Los Angeles to Chicago. You stop, things happen, you adjust. You set out to do something and things happen. Your partner has needs, and you must adjust to them. You learn, you listen, you change, you experience. You are different at the end, because of the journey.

If you take such a hard position in the scene that no movement is possible – if you say, "I want this, nothing will stop me" – the danger is that nothing will happen to you. Playing a scene is doing something to get what you want, but, it is also what happens to you while you try to get it. You cannot dismiss the other person.

A note on becoming an actor

The Neighborhood Playhouse School of the Theatre was and is a professional school for serious students of acting. When I was interviewed and then accepted, I was informed early on that if I could not keep up with their curriculum, I would be asked to leave.

The School has an excellent reputation. In the 1950s, when I attended, Sandy Meisner (his name was Sanford, but everyone called him Sandy) was our extraordinary teacher of acting technique, the incomparable Martha Graham taught us dance and movement, and Evangeline Machlin taught speech, using her excellent text, *Speech for the Stage*. David Pressman taught us improvisation and Wynn Handman began his teaching career by assisting Sandy. It was a good place to learn.

In the first year of the two-year program we had speech, dance, acting, and improvisation classes six days a week. We worked on exercises to develop the senses, to heighten our ability to really listen and really focus. We learned that you must always be specific.

In the second year we performed a variety of scenes. We read entire plays and broke their scenes down into actions and objectives. We performed these scenes in the Playhouse Theatre. Fellow students, invited guests, and faculty were our audience. Sandy took notes and usually gave a critique after each presentation.

I was assigned a very complex scene from a play called *The Father*, by August Strindberg. My character was named the Captain. He is in the cavalry, is a strict, disciplined perfectionist, and has an obsession with his child. The way I saw it, to my character, the child represents his conception of immortality. He says, "I want to be her teacher," and "I want to give her my soul." He believes that if the child is taken away from him, he will die.

His wife Laura wants to keep and control the child. She plants the seed of doubt in his mind. She says, "Bertha is my child, but not yours."

The Captain sets out to prove he is the father. Having a scientific mind, he must get 100 percent proof. In the end, he cannot prove it and this is what destroys him.

One thought took hold of me. If Sandy and the faculty were not satisfied with my progress, they could ask me to leave the school. So I stayed up all night. I read the play again. Then I focused on the scene. My spine was to prove I am the father. My objective was to get evidence. Why? To remove any doubt in my mind. I approached the scene as if my life depended on it. On my list of actions were:

- to question the nurse
- to instruct the nurse
- to study the magazine

- to examine the photograph album
- to ask a point of law
- to question the doctor
- to challenge the doctor
- to triumphantly tell my stories about two women I met who were not completely honest.

The next morning, having had little sleep, I appeared at the Playhouse Theatre. It was crowded with students, faculty, and friends. Sandy was sitting near the front, taking notes. When our scene was called, the student playing the doctor, the woman playing the nurse, and I got onto the stage, looked at each other, and took a deep breath, remembering our preparation for the scene. Then Sandy's assistant said something like, "Start the scene," and we began.

It felt good to finally say my words. My actions were now clear and strong, and my objective in the scene kept my energy up. As the scene went along, I grew more demanding and passionate. I looked forward to the next action with great anticipation. And, I must say, I particularly enjoyed condemning the ladies in my two stories about unfaithful women. (Having read the entire play, I knew that the Captain becomes more violent, is put into a straight jacket, and finally collapses and dies. This scene put my character on the path to destruction.)

After the scene was over, there was applause and then Sandy Meisner slowly stood up and said, "Well, Mr. Ruscio," – long pause – "I think," – another pause – "you might become an actor."[3] I heard cheering from my buddies and fellow students.

For several days, those words rang in my ears. They gave me the courage to go out and pursue my career. *So therefore*, and thanks to Sandy Meisner, I became an actor.

17

PREPARATION

When you come on stage, your life has already begun. You cannot come on the stage dry. You must be able to answer these questions before you enter.

- Where did I come from?
- How long have I been gone?
- What have I been doing?
- Why did I come here?
- What do I expect to find going on here?
- What do I want to do about it?
- Do I expect to succeed or fail in my action?
- Does this moment advance me towards the thing I want most in life?

Within any scene, you can always find your point of personal contact, what it means to you. From the dominant emotional circumstances, you must find your essence; that is your preparation.

Preparation essentially is talking to yourself to stimulate the process of imagination prior to coming into the scene. It is autosuggestion. It is getting the emotional juices flowing to stimulate the proper behavior just before entering a scene.

In Strindberg's play *The Father*, the title character enters to find out certain things about his daughter. His wife has told him that he is not really the father of the child. The child is his conception of immortality: take her away from him and you destroy him. This is what happens in the play.

First, you must understand that this is a certain kind of man: strict, proud, a perfectionist. The child is his life: she means everything to him.

To prepare for this scene, you must imagine the most important person in your life – it could be your mother, father, wife or husband, son or daughter. You must concentrate on that person until, for you, they embody your world, your life, your emotional essence.

You talk to yourself: "They can't take her away from me! Oh my God – what will I do without her? She means everything to me!" Then, when you come on stage and ask about your child, the emotion of a real experience has taken hold of you. And you are prepared for the experience of the scene.

The key question in all preparation is: *What does it mean to me?*

A note on emotional preparation

When I played the role of Sitting Bull, the great Native American chief, in Arthur Kopit's *Indians*, I faced a special problem of preparation. Here was a man whose people were being systematically destroyed. They were starving and dying on the reservations. In one crucial scene, the old man speaks to American government representatives about his people, his hopes for his people, the land, and their vision.

But when I researched the life of Sitting Bull, I discovered that he once toured with Buffalo Bill as part of the Wild West Show. And, in that capacity, he had to don lavish Native American costumes and dance and the people laughed at his antics. I began to realize how, deep down inside, this man was ashamed of what he had to do to survive and make money for his people.

When, in the play, he spoke to the government representatives, there was irony and sarcasm in his voice: "Therefore, tell the Great Father that if he wishes us to live like White men, we will do so. Therefore, tell him for me that I have never yet seen a White man starving, so he should send us food so we can live like the White man."[1]

Once I found the irony and the sarcasm, I found the preparation, and I was well on my way to finding the character.

In that note I was speaking, of course, of emotional preparation. There is also physical preparation, where you prepare your body offstage prior to your entrance so that when you enter, we see a human being in a situation responding naturally. As the great man said: "Suit the action to the word."[2]

You cannot come on stage dry, nor can you come on stage cold. The great English actor Edmund Kean, prior to his entrances in *King Lear*, would literally shake the rafters and rattle the boards in the wings. When he entered, you saw a man whose emotional and physical juices were flowing.

Sometimes I have seen actors sitting quietly prior to their entrance, mentally and spiritually crossing the bridge from reality to make-believe. Sometimes actors will try a combination of physical, emotional, and spiritual preparations. Prior to their entrance, some actors like to do pushups to get the blood moving. I have seen some very good actors running around backstage, talking in character to anyone there, trying to get their imaginary lives going.

It would be foolish to argue the relative merits of these kinds of work because any system which helps the actor give a truthful performance is beneficial.

In class work, prior to a scene or exercise, prepare: warm up your creative instrument. Ask and answer the vital questions.

- Where have I just come from?
- Where am I going now?
- What do I want?
- What does this mean to me?
- What is the emotional essence of this scene?
- What is my personal element?
- What must I do just before entering this scene to stimulate the proper behavior?

Ideally, preparation, when perfected, should be reduced to a minimum of time and effort. But for class work you should do everything that is possible, before words are necessary. The words are the result of a certain experience. Preparation provides you with the essence and stimuli of that experience. When you enter the scene you have physically, mentally, and emotionally built a foundation, filled in the past, as it were, from which you may go forward naturally.

Another note on preparation

Here's a story describing a very different aspect of preparation. When I was a young man growing up in New England, I really enjoyed watching basketball games and my favorite team was the Boston Celtics. They kept winning championships and one of my heroes was Bob Cousy. He could do things with a basketball that amazed me. During my research for this book, I came across an article which has to do with preparation. The article was in *Cavalier* magazine and it recounted how Cousy, a star on those Celtics teams, prepared for a big game.

> It's the only way I can get myself up for a game – I've got to pick out a guy on the other team and start thinking about how he is going to try to make me look bad. I'll lock myself in a room all day and concentrate on the one player. When I'm through, I can hate him pretty good. Then I can go out and play at my best against him. It's a trick, sure it is. But if I don't do it, then I just run through the motions. That isn't right.[3]

So, you see, even great athletes prepare for their entrances.

Preparation exercises

How would you prepare for the following situations?

- You have just been told by your closest friends that the ghost of your dead father was seen last night. You agree to go with them tonight to try to speak to the ghost (Hamlet in Shakespeare's *Hamlet*).
- You believe you are ugly and will be an old maid. A charming con man has defended you in front of your brothers. You do not trust him, yet you are fascinated by him. You visit him while he sleeps, bringing blankets to him (Liza in N. Richard Nash's *The Rainmaker*).

- You are ambitious to be Queen of Scotland. King Duncan will be a guest in your house tonight. Your husband would like to be king, but seems to be afraid of murder. You talk to him to persuade him to "be a man" (Lady Macbeth in Shakespeare's *Macbeth*).

- You are an amateur actor who has an opportunity to star in a play. You would like to play all the parts. You must convince the director of your brilliant talent (Bottom in Shakespeare's *A Midsummer Night's Dream*).

- Your husband used to be a brilliant actor. Now he is an alcoholic. He begins to doubt his talent. You want to put him on his feet so you can break away and make your own life. You have a throbbing toothache, but must confront a young director who doesn't trust you (Georgie in Clifford Odets's *Country Girl*).

- You are a happy, gregarious longshoreman. You live with your wife and niece. Now the niece has fallen in love with an immigrant. Subconsciously you desire the niece for yourself. You invent arguments against this immigrant. You visit a friendly attorney and try to get him to help you (Eddie in Arthur Miller's *A View from the Bridge*).

- You lost everything. Now you come to your sister's home to visit and get a hold of yourself. You are on the verge of a nervous breakdown. You discover your sister's husband is a boor and there is no room for you in their home (Blanche in Tennessee Williams's *A Streetcar Named Desire*).

- You were a captain in the army. You lost most of your men. You feel guilty and cannot reach out to take material possessions. You also feel awkward about your dead brother's girl, whom you now love. She announces she is leaving. You must make her understand your special problem (Chris in Arthur Miller's *All My Sons*).

- You are a dutiful wife. Your husband had an affair with the cleaning girl. Now she has become powerful and would like to destroy you. Your husband can help you if he publicly denounces her. You must get his assistance (Elizabeth in Arthur Miller's *The Crucible*).

- You are a dope addict. Your wife thinks you are cheating with another woman. You must make her believe it is not another woman, but are too ashamed to tell her the truth (Johnny in Michael Gazzo's *A Hatful of Rain*).

- Every day you come to Central Park to sit on a bench and read and relax. Today, a nervous young man is there and insists it is his bench and challenges you to fight for it (Peter in Edward Albee's *The Zoo Story*).
- You believe in God, but he has taken away all your wealth and good fortune. Your children are dead. Your wife has deserted you. You are destitute and your skin is infected with disease. You are partially blind and lame. Now you turn to God and demand an explanation (J. B. in Archibald MacLeish's *J. B.*).
- You are a witch-boy who falls in love with a beautiful woman. You want to be a human. You want to discover human beings and their ways. You plead with the other witches to let you be human (John in Howard Richardson and William Berney's *Dark of the Moon*).
- Thieves are destroying Paris. You call your friends together and conduct a trial, seeking justice (the Countess Aurelia in Jean Giraudoux's *The Madwoman of Chaillot*).
- You believe your wife is trying to have you committed to an insane asylum. The only way you can prevent it is to cooperate with her, though you no longer love her (Jim in Joseph Kramm's *The Shrike*).
- The man you love writes poems on trees proclaiming his love for you. You are disguised as a young boy. You meet him in the forest. You decide to play a game with him – a mock courtship (Rosalind in Shakespeare's *As You Like It*).
- You are a brave and stubborn Native American leader who has just been told to keep quiet in front of your people. They look to you to respond to a government representative who questions your right to own the land. You were a great warrior, but now you must be a statesman (Sitting Bull in Arthur Kopit's *Indians*).
- You are a blustery king and soldier who must woo a shy French queen and persuade her to marry you. You can barely speak French. She speaks very little English (Henry in Shakespeare's *Henry V*).
- You have killed Lady Anne's father and husband. Now she is en route to the burial ground, weeping. She knows you are the murderer. You are convinced you must woo her and make her your wife. You stop the funeral procession and woo her (Richard in Shakespeare's *Richard III*).

Plays abound in fascinating situations. What *as ifs* can you use to make these situations real to you? What preparation – mental, physical, emotional – must you make to enter and play these scenes? What experiences in your own life will stimulate the proper behavior to make these imaginary circumstances come alive?

18

SCENES

There are hundreds of plays that you should see and read. These plays contain excellent scenes for you to experiment with and develop your technique. You should work on all kinds of scenes: contemporary, classical, tragedies, comedies, farces, and melodramas. Each scene will present a new challenge for you.

Using the actors' worksheet, work on a variety of scenes. Select one character and extract the acting elements.

Begin by using the words *I want*, *I must*, etc. – this will help you to cross the bridge into that character.

- List your objective in the scene: what you want.
- List your reasons: why you want what you want.
- List your actions: what you do to get what you want.
- Add the *as ifs*: the way you intend to get what you want.
- Add your personal connection: the unique emotional element.

As you work on the scene, you will also discover a way to prepare for the scene. Naturally, read the play first. Determine what the play is about. Discover its spine. Determine the spine of your character. If you cannot read the entire play and you are working on a scene, you must make choices. You cannot act on *maybe*. You must *will* what you do.

Learn all you can about the play and the character, and make as complete an analysis as you can. Even if the choices you make are wrong, in relation to our work here, it is better to have wrong choices than no choices at all. You must select the spines before the scene can start working for you.

As you work on scenes, change the actions, mix up the *as ifs*, try different personal connections. Use these scenes to develop your technique. Pretend the scene is a picture puzzle and, always remembering the total picture, that you can extract one piece, sharpen it, give it definition, play with it, as it were, and still place it back in its proper spot in relation to the whole picture.

This way, soon, you can approach and master any scene you work on as a craftsperson.

Actor's worksheet

Name of play _____

Spine of play _____

_____

My name _____

My spine (What do I want?) _____

_____

Why do I want it? _____

_____

How will I attempt to get it? (My *as if*) _____

_____

My preparation _____

_____

My objective in this scene _____

_____

Why? _____

_____

As if? _____

_____

My actions in this scene (the things I do):

Action one _____
   Why? _____
   How? _____
   My preparation _____

Action two _____
   Why? _____
   How? _____
   My preparation _____

Action three _____
   Why? _____
   How? _____
   My preparation _____

Action four _____
   Why? _____
   How? _____
   My preparation _____

Action five _____
   Why? _____
   How? _____
   My preparation _____

Part 3

THE PLAY

19

INTRODUCTION

You have been cast in a play and are told, "We begin rehearsals in one week" or "in six weeks we open!"

What do you do?

You are an artist who must approach the craft of acting with the same dedication and working technique as other artists. But you are dealing with the art of make-believe. You must literally transform yourself into another person. And you have a deadline to meet.

Remember, the theatre is always *now*. And when you accept a role you've said, in effect, "I know my business; I can deliver."

So, how do you approach this role?

Let's begin. The play rests before you. What do you do?

20

READ THE PLAY

First, read the play

This may seem obvious, but you would be surprised by how many actors have not read the entire play before coming to the first rehearsal.

Read the play through at one sitting and try to capture a general understanding of it, a flavor, an intuitive feeling. Rely on your instinct. Forget that you will act in it – just read it objectively.

Do you find it challenging?

If something doesn't attract you, chances are you won't enjoy it or want to spend time on it. I realize that many times you cannot hand-pick your roles, but if you can, the general rule applies: if you don't like the play, don't do it.

However, if something in the play attracts you, holds your interest, that is good. Now, wait a day or two and ...

21

THE MAIN IDEA AND SPECIAL QUALITY

... read the play again

As you read the play this second time, read for intellectual comprehension. What is the main idea of this play? What is this play about? A play is never about nothing. You should be able to say:

- This is a play about three sisters yearning to return to Moscow (*The Three Sisters* by Anton Chekhov).
- This is a play about a boy trying to leave home without hurting his parents (*Leaving Home* by David French).
- This is a play about the great suffering and faith of one man (*J. B.* by Archibald MacLeish).
- This is a play about a former star, with a weakness for alcohol and men, who tries to straighten out her life (*The Gingerbread Lady* by Neil Simon).

Whatever the main idea is, you should be able to express it in a sentence or two. If you still like the play, wait another day or two and then ...

... read it a third time

As you read the play this time, read it like an actor searching for your point of personal identification, understanding, connection. Seek the special quality of this play.

What is the main idea the playwright is exploring? Why did he or she write the play? Is he or she exploring:

+ the absurdity of life? What does the play say about it?
+ the grandeur and meaning of life?
+ one feature of the complexity of life?
+ family relationships?

Is this play a drama, a comedy, a farce, a tragedy? Is it contemporary or classical? Is this a new play or one already proven? As an actor you may need this information so you can properly play your role. For example, for a proven play, you may want to research prior productions. And you may want to be able to discuss the play with the director and your fellow actors. The director will ask questions about your view of the play and the characters. You must be prepared to take part in this creative process.

22

THE CLIMAX

Pay special attention to the climax of your play. The climax is the highest point of tension, when the basic conflict reaches its ultimate height and begins to descend. Worthington Miner, an American director in the 1920s and 1930s, expresses it this way:

> A play is a preamble to a climax and that climax must be the consummate statement of the play's intention ... it is the completion of a statement regarding some selected human beings in a cycle of selected circumstances.[1]

The climax will tell you how far your character is willing to go to achieve his or her objective. Does he or she back off? Or go all the way?

In *A View from the Bridge*, Eddie Carbone begins a series of actions from which he cannot extricate himself and he goes all the way – to death – before the play ends.

See your character in the midst of these given circumstances. What special appeal is there about this character? Can you see him or her as they move in and out of the scenes of this play? Can you empathize with this character? Do you care what happens to this imaginary person? Is this character unique? What special problems does this role present?

Ask yourself, "What must I do to myself in order to do what this character does in this situation?" Already you've put together three elements necessary to approaching this role:

1   You've found the play challenging.
2   You've learned what the play is about.
3   You've found the climax and the special quality of this play and this character.

Before rehearsals begin you will add two more elements:

4   a character analysis
5   the spine of your character.

23

CHARACTER ANALYSIS

On a separate sheet, list your:

- place in time
- age in years
- heredity
- profession
- likes and dislikes
- temperament and psychology
- physical, mental, and emotional traits
- walk and speech habits
- attire
- view of the world and how you see yourself in it.

Refer to Chapter 9, Life Studies, in Part 1 to help you fill in these characteristics and identify the unique elements of this character you are playing.

24

THE SPINE OF YOUR CHARACTER

Discover the spine of your character.

In the Canadian play *Leaving Home* by David French, we have the story of blocked affections in a family far removed from home. A family has moved from Newfoundland to Toronto and they tease, accuse, avoid, and torture each other. The father needles and abuses the eldest boy mercilessly. The climax occurs when the father realizes that his son loves him very much. The father, doing a turnabout, pleads with his son to stay. The son, however, must leave home. He needs to find his own life. He is in danger of being smothered at home. This is what the boy wants: *to leave home without hurting my parents.* This is his spine.

What is your life goal? What is your basic psychological, spiritual drive and desire, the thing you fundamentally want most of all?

Find out how your spine relates to what the play is about. If the play is about people who cannot communicate and you *want to leave home without hurting my parents*, then you can see the basic conflict of your character: trying to make people understand what you must do and why.

Again, in *Leaving Home* the father accidentally finds out about his son's leaving and we have a whole new violent turn in the action. Now there is a confrontation. But the son resolutely pursues his spine: he must leave; there is no turning back now. So he endures tears, insults, pleadings, threats, even whippings; but he goes. He achieves his goal. He gets what he wants. And he was willing to go all the way to do so.

So, ideally, when you go to the first rehearsal, you should have five fundamentals in place:

1   You like the play.
2   You know what the play is about.
3   You have found the climax and the special quality of this play and this character.
4   You have written a character analysis and explored the uniqueness of your character.
5   You have discovered what your character wants – your spine – and you know how far you're willing to go to get it.

Here's an example of an actor finding his character's spine. I was working on the film *Al Capone* at Allied Artists. Rod Steiger was playing the title role. Steiger was a leading method actor of the day along with Marlon Brando, Steve McQueen, and a few others, and was known for his passionate portrayals. I accidentally picked up his script and saw that he had written and underlined on page one, "to own everything." I didn't realize it at the time, but now I know that was his spine for the character.

25

REHEARSALS BEGIN

The rehearsal period is a special time in the daily life of actors. A time for serious and creative work. Be alert physically, mentally, and emotionally. Remember, the director has worked on the play prior to rehearsals. He or she will express his or her ideas. Other actors will contribute as well. Be open to suggestions at these rehearsals.

During the first readings:

1   Listen to the play. The other actors will bring elements you could never imagine reading the play alone, so listen as though for the first time. Observe and try to drink in the play.

2   Find the objects of concentration. In *Leaving Home*, the boy's high school diploma plays an important role in the action. The father asks about it early. He brags about it, shows it off and finally, in a fit of anger, destroys it. So the diploma is one object of concentration for actors.

3   Find the logical connections from beat to beat. As you hear the play, notice how one idea leads naturally and progressively to the next. Your character will develop like that, beat by beat, naturally.

4   Take an active part in the group process of exploring the play. This taking part has several aspects:

   +   Make notes of observation in your script. Use a pencil with an eraser.
   +   Explore the meaning of the play with the director and your fellow actors.

+ Explore your spine with the director and how it relates to the meaning of the play.
+ Discuss the contribution of each character to the meaning of the play.
+ Discuss the conflicts of each character.
+ Discuss relationships and change of such relationships during the course of the play.
+ Study sketches and ground plans of the set and costumes; they will help you locate your character in the proper setting.

After the early readings, a general agreement is reached by the actors and the director concerning what the play is about and the approach to rehearsals. You will usually then receive a rehearsal schedule.

26

ELEMENTS OF CHARACTERIZATION

Now begins the second phase of rehearsals. After the early reading sessions are over and prior to your blocking sessions, go home and:

1 Study your character analysis.
2 Begin working on the elements that are special to your character. For example, what do you wear? Why? How do you walk? Why? Jeff Corey talked in his classes about an old wino he was studying. This man walked very delicately, as if he were almost afraid to move. This gave the man a shuffling, tentative rhythm. Jeff realized that the man had probably wet his trousers and it hurt him to walk because he was sore, and that explained his peculiar shuffling.

Once, in Pennsylvania during a season of summer stock (where you rehearse one play during the day and perform another play every night), I found myself wearing a different hat each Monday morning as we would begin rehearsing a new play. This helped me to find my new character.

As Laurence Olivier taught:

> You must constantly observe: a walk, a limp, a run; how a head inclines to one side when listening; the twitch of an eyebrow; the hand that picks the nose when it thinks no one is looking; the mustache puller; the eyes that never look at you; the nose that sniffs long after the cold is gone.[1]

3   Review your spine.
4   Break down the role. This is the heart of your work and has several aspects:

   + Scenes: number these.
   + Objectives: find what you want in each scene.
   + Motivations: decide why you want what you want.
   + Actions: what you do to get what you want. List and describe these actions in pencil on the side of the script.
   + *As ifs*: the particular way you intend to execute your actions. These will come more readily as you begin rehearsals, but you should have a general idea of how you want to play your actions at this point.
   + Personal connections: key emotional memories and images may enter your mind. Write them down. During rehearsals, you will attempt to include them in your work.
   + Beats (units of action of each scene): these will indicate a change of direction, the entrance of a new character, a new subject, etc.

5   Answer the following questions:

   + What are the given circumstances of each scene?
   + What has happened just prior to the scene?
   + Where are the transitions?
   + What must be my preparation for each scene?

6   Write your notes on the side of your script where you can refer to them during rehearsals. This information will change also, but it will give you guidelines as you begin to develop your character.

27

THE USE OF IMPROVISATION

It is during this period, before your lines are memorized and while you are still searching for the character, that some teachers and directors employ improvisation. Improvisation can be helpful in a number of ways.

Focus and believability

Here is a portion of a letter I received from a student, referring to my directing.

> He emphasized "acting is believing" and worked you until something believable happened. One anecdotal story: My first role as Joan of Arc in *The Lark*. We were on the jail scene and he said he didn't believe that I saw Saint Michael. He then took off his coat and threw it over my head. He said there it would stay until he believed in what I was saying. I am not sure how many rehearsals I had that coat over my head, but, in retrospect, I learned how to focus, engage in the reality of the given circumstance. Then, finally, I saw Saint Michael. The coat came off and tears streamed down his face and he said, "Now I believe you."[1]

That student was Anne Seward Hansen who became a television star, appearing on *As the World Turns* for many years.

Particularization

A young actress in one of my classes was playing a scene in which she was describing to her girlfriend what it would be like to go to Hollywood and become an actress. She had just received a letter and she was reading it to that girlfriend. Somehow, the scene was too earthbound. To help her particularize the scene, I suggested that she was Cinderella at the ball, dancing with Prince Charming, laughing and singing, uninhibited and free. I told her to forget the lines in the script, just celebrate this delicious moment.

She took off. Suddenly she came alive, laughing and dancing around the room. Her girlfriend joined her in the laughter and together we discovered two young, bright girls fully relishing a completely ecstatic moment. That made the scene. We transformed all the blocking and this scene became one of the highlights of the play.

Music and images

A young actor was performing a scene from a movie in which he came into the home of a writer and his wife. Together with two friends he proceeded to tie up the writer, destroy the home, and leave. This was a good actor, but the scene lacked a hook and attitude, a dark comic aspect that would make the scene come alive in a special way. We improvised. The actor was to play as if he were a bird, a shrike. The shrike is a relaxed creature, cool and composed, which can suddenly become violent. We found music by Bach and played it in the background during the scene.

This time the actor entered, smiled, almost priest-like, asking for assistance. He spoke in soft tones. You believed him, you liked him. Suddenly he leaped upon the writer, deftly slashed him, laughing in a sick and fascinating way. Then he tied him up and slowly moved toward the wife. With deliberate, almost surgical speed he moved the wife behind the sofa and assaulted her. In balletic fashion he meticulously destroyed the papers, turned over the furniture, threw down the books and lamps, and so on. Then he left, engulfed in maniacal joy. We transformed the image of the shrike and justified the music in the background throughout the scene when it was finally performed.

As ifs

Once, while working on a scene from *The Subject Was Roses* by Frank Gilroy, I helped my student improvise the moment when the parents and son return home, slightly inebriated. They improvised the entire scene as if they were on the stage of a burlesque house, telling bawdy jokes. The actors invented a song and dance routine. The mother, who was sober and wanted to go to bed, resisted joining the two men, but they insisted. She went along with it for a while. Finally, she broke away. The two men, father and son, continued telling jokes like old troupers. They finally collapsed and giggled and stumbled off to bed. The improvisation freed the actors physically and loosened them up emotionally.

Obstacles

You can bring in an element that proves an obstacle for your character to make your improvisation more challenging. This obstacle can be emotional, physical, or psychological. Here are a few obstacle improvisations.

- You must tell a friend some bad news. Obstacle: your friend has a severe heart condition.
- You are saying goodbye to your parents. Obstacle: you don't really want to go.
- You have just won a big role in a movie. Obstacle: you don't want to upset your close friend who tried out for the same role.
- You are giving a lecture. Obstacle: there is something in your eye.
- You are telling friends your success story. Obstacle: your wife, who is in the room, knows you are lying and you know she knows.

28

BLOCKING SESSIONS

First, take your time. This is a period of close collaboration between you the actor, the director, and your fellow actors.

This period is terribly important because the actor is moving and trying to find the simple reality of the lines. In this period, you must find out what you can believe, how you will behave, and what you will experience. You will also begin to test your actions.

This is a delicate period and the actor must not be rushed into a movement or a piece of blocking just to accommodate an impatient director or an aggressive actor. The actor must try to work for a flow of movement which relates to his or her understanding of the character. The actor is questioning how and why he or she would move in a certain way and at a particular time.

Now try your actions. Explore with your director and your fellow actors your objectives in the scene. Remember, each move must be motivated. A cross or a piece of business or any movement must have a reason behind it. And that reason must be consistent with your character. A line is dead until something happens to give it life; it is the same with the movement. Maybe it is some information you have just heard or the entrance of a new character or important news; whatever it is, it must exist.

Consider these two basic principles from Sandy Meisner: "First, don't do anything unless something happens to make you do it. Second, what you do doesn't depend on you; it depends on the other fellow."[1]

In the early blocking period you are trying to fit pieces of a huge jigsaw puzzle together. Take the time to be correct in your choices. It is better to discuss a questionable move now and change it, if necessary, than to wait until close to opening night when other elements will weigh too heavily on the director and cast for you to examine these choices with them.

A moment is heightened, a transition is effective, a pause has rich meaning, if your blocking and movement is clear, motivated, and relates to your intention in the scene. Blocking should not be just pretty pictures and composition or clever movement; it should be a justified, selected activity which comes from the actor's awareness of the given circumstances of the play.

When you begin blocking Act 1, you would be wise to have worked on that act prior to rehearsals and know your actions and objectives. Know where your actions change, where your transitions occur. Your blocking will help you perform the actions fully and interestingly, but you must do your homework first. If you have chosen to tease your boyfriend at a given moment, you may want to delay a cross to make your point with him. During the blocking sessions, if you are testing your actions, not only will they help make the play come alive, but a good director will work with you to make your character truthful and unique.

1   Remember, every move and every word must be motivated by your character. With script still in hand, you are exploring these questions as you play your actions, testing and adjusting along the way. You are asking yourself:

   + What actions lead toward my goal?
   + What actions lead away from my goal?
   + How do my actions affect the other characters?
   + How do my actions affect the plot?
   + How do my actions affect the blocking?
   + Have I chosen the proper actions for this scene?

2   You are defining relationships. In specific detail, go through each character in the play and describe your actions and reactions to them, scene by scene.

   + What is my relationship to the other people in the play?
   + Do I like or dislike them? Why?
   + How do these relationships affect my actions?

3   You are experimenting with particular ways of playing your actions.

   + What is my image? My adjustment? My *as if*?
   + What is my attitude?
   + Should I play this moment as if I were an animal?
   + How many different ways can I play this scene?
   + Which way is the proper way?

4   You are working with emotion.

   + What is the emotional essence of this scene?
   + Do I need a personal connection for this scene to come alive?
   + Can I use an emotional recall exercise to stimulate the necessary emotion?
   + Have I ever been in this situation before? What was the dominant feeling at that moment?

5   Underscore character-revealing lines and objects of concentration. Remember, most scenes have a progression and a top. Find the high moment of the scene. Generally, the strongest actions will occur near the end of the scene.

6   Concentrate on the climax of the play.

   + What do you do at this high point in the play?
   + What is your objective?
   + What are your major actions during the climactic scene of the play? Everything you have built should lead to this moment. You may want to change some actions, test a new objective, review your spine. The climax should reveal the ultimate decision of your character. The thing you want most in life will be tested at the climax. Build for that moment.

29

DETAILED WORK ON EACH ACT

The blocking sessions are completed. Now the director will take you through the play, one act at a time, as he or she tries to bring the entire play into focus. It is at this point that the director will work on such elements as:

- climaxes, large and small; sustaining interest and excitement from scene to scene, progressively building to the main climax
- variety
- improving the composition; using the stage areas carefully, not overworking one area
- units of the act, especially exits and entrances.

Usually, after detailed work, directors will run through the entire act. As the director begins to mold the play, you the actor, in your deepening involvement during this period, must memorize your lines.

Some actors learn the lines of each act soon after it's blocked. Others prefer to learn each act before it is blocked. Others learn their dialogue as the blocking sessions occur, simultaneously learning the lines as they relate to the blocking and business of the play. Experienced actors sometimes memorize the entire play before rehearsals begin. (I do not recommend this method, except in emergencies.)

Once your lines are memorized and the script is out of hand, you begin working on a different level. You begin to see the other characters; your hands are free to gesture and use props fully; your sensory equipment is heightened; and a new physical and emotional freedom enters into your playing.

A good director will now clarify and select. He or she will inspire you to play a moment more fully, to take a pause, to add a cross, to fill out a moment. And you will be ready to experience more fully the action of the scene.

As you get off-book and make that transition from reading to experiencing, you will be concerned with enriching the role. You'll begin to:

- work for timing of business and precision of movement
- work for clarity, emphasis, and variety
- decide which are plot lines, character lines, theme lines
- work on preparation prior to each entrance
- begin wearing costume pieces and accessories
- begin using hand props
- begin each act with proper attack
- end each act with somewhere to go.

In other words, at any moment in the rehearsal, you the actor should know:

- who you are and where you are
- where you came from
- what you are doing there
- why you came here
- what you expected to find here
- what you came here to do, why, and how
- if you expect to succeed in this action and why
- if this moment leads towards your objective in the play and how.

You should know your actions and objective in each scene. You should also know how you intend to play each action and why. And, you should be flexible enough to change an action or a way of playing an action whenever the growth of your character demands it. You must always keep in view your overall objective – your spine – the overarching thing you want. As Laurence Olivier is reported to have said, "The actor must be absolutely clear in his mind where he is going."[1]

30

RUN-THROUGHS

This is a hectic period of trying to fit all the pieces of this gigantic puzzle together. First run-throughs are notorious for their confusion. Suddenly, you feel like a baby elephant trying to walk, falling over your own feet. You discover the trees are there, but you cannot see the forest. Though one or two moments are working, you cannot grasp the entire character. You feel you are talking too fast; the lines and the actions are not meshing. The play is out of sync.

But, certain things do begin to take shape. Some actions are playing fully. Your relationship to other characters is defined. The elements of character you selected earlier are beginning to work. You have built your scenes carefully, so the small climaxes are beginning to come alive. You are emotionally free, so tears and laughter come at the proper moments. And, you kept your eye on the objective during that long, difficult scene. You are different when the scene is over. Something happened to you. You are much more secure than you think.

Granted, the addition of music and sound cues, the pieces of costume and props and other technical elements have added new adjustments, but, within all this, *you played your action*!

You knew what you wanted and what you had to do and you went out and did it. You attacked each new beat with fresh energy. And, above all, you kept in mind your super desire, the element that gives you thrust and direction – your spine. This spine gave you the capacity and direction to tie it all together.

If you have numbered your scenes and you appear in eight scenes, this spine will provide the unity of purpose, the glue, the overriding element that identifies and pulls each scene together. Suddenly, scene 3, though it is not a powerful scene, takes its proper perspective, in relation to scene 6. Scene 2 sets up scene 5, and so on.

You, as an actor, now have tracks to ride on, guidelines to follow. For example, you might know as you approach scene 1 that your objective is to get information and you know why and how. You know your actions are to flatter, to question, to tell a story, to persuade, to insist, and to threaten. You have rehearsed these actions. You have selected them. Now remains experiencing them – each night – as though it is the first time.

You will struggle through these first run-throughs.

Your task is to believe every line, behave truthfully in every situation, begin experiencing the role emotionally, physically, and spiritually. After the run-through, the director will give notes to the company. He or she will be concerned with the overall play – *is the story being told*?

The director's notes may concern:

- loss of spontaneity
- variety
- builds and diminishes
- shift of emphasis
- line emphasis
- physical actions and non-verbal behavior (business)
- exits and entrances
- props, costumes, cues.

Adjustments

Within the overall understanding of your character, you should be able to make any adjustment at this time without weakening the fabric you've created since the first rehearsal.

You must be concerned now with *fresh stimuli*.

- You may have to find new images to stimulate the proper behavior in a scene.
- Some scenes will work. Others will have to be bigger, richer, or quieter and subtler.

- You may be too strong in an early scene, so you may have to cut back, always justifying your behavior.
- You may need fresh attacks to some scenes.
- You may need new *as ifs* or emotional stimuli.

You must also be able to hold your concentration.

- Listen as if you are hearing the words for the first time.
- Listen as the character would listen. React as the character would react. What does this line mean to me?
- Concentrate, listen, think, react fully.
- Trust the material. Remember, you like this play and it has a special meaning for you.
- Remember, this is not simple reality, it is theatrical reality because the stage is theatrical life, sharply defined, selected, heightened.

31

FINAL RUN-THROUGHS

Now you begin the exciting days of seeing the pieces fit together. Your house is beginning to take shape. It is solid brick. The foundation – your spine – is strong. The rooms of your house – your objectives – are well built. The furniture and appliances – your actions – are new and guaranteed. The colors – the *as ifs* – you've chosen are rich and comfortable. The pictures on the walls, the decorations and accessories, your personal touches, reflect taste and elegance.

You can move from one room to another and enjoy the scenery, secure in the knowledge that this is a unique house, a one-and-only house, created by your very special talent.

Now we add:

- the completed sets and the set crews
- complete costumes, properties, and furniture
- light cues and sound cues
- special effects
- backstage crew and personnel.

All of these newly added elements will seem to take away from your performance. For example:

- your concentration may be diverted
- your full playing and involvement may be diluted
- your emotional freedom may be blocked
- your movements and business may be hampered.

The addition of lights and sound and set, the technical adjustments, plus the need to project and clarify your role, may frustrate you during this period. But soon you will accept these elements in their proper perspective, as part of the theatricality of the presentation, and you will use them. Here are a few personal observations to help you through this process.

Generally, not enough time is spent with the actors to acquaint them with the stage and guarantee they are at home with the set, properties, lights, sound, costumes, and makeup. Actors and the director should insist on time to move around their house – to get to know where they live.

Unless the actor is at home on that stage, unless he or she is secure in his or her makeup and costume, the play will never come alive. My teacher, Sandy Meisner, used to say, "the only king and ruler of the stage is the talented actor."[1] I would add the king must be comfortable and secure in his home and costume and settings.

The actor must rehearse in his or her costumes and makeup, use the properties and move about on the completed set, until he or she belongs there. Nothing is as embarrassing as a company that rehearses six weeks and then spends two days in costumes and one day on the set. They cannot help looking newly-starched and awkward. The stage is where the actor lives and you should spend the time necessary on it to become completely secure.

Years ago, I was acting in a play called *Geniuses* by Jonathan Reynolds. My character, Bart Keely, was a vigorous, aggressive man who styled himself after Ernest Hemingway, beard and all. In Act 3 the beard is removed. After the play I asked my son Michael, "How did you like the play?" He replied, "Dad, when you lost your beard, you also lost your character."[2] And he was right: I was not completely secure.

Tommaso Salvini, an Italian actor and a great Othello, used to arrive at the theatre many hours before the curtain was to rise. He would prepare his soul for the performance. He would apply makeup and part of his costume and walk about the stage – move around his house – to get at one with the set and furniture. He'd then go back to the dressing room, add another costume piece, and return to the stage, this time more fully concentrated on his task: to prepare his soul and mind and body for the audience. By the time the curtain rose, he was ready; this was his home.

Figure 7
Al, in *Geniuses*,
with the infamous
Hemingway beard.

So, actors: be selfish about your set, your costumes, your makeup, your character. Protect them.

During these final run-throughs, try to sense the entire potential of the role, from beginning to end. Some scenes, you will discover, are working marvelously and you sense they are nearly complete and realized. Work until all your scenes are rich and unique and truthful. And try to capture the essence of your character by experiencing fully each time. Never be afraid to make a change if it develops in the performance of the role. Acting is made up of impulses and instincts and you must dare to follow your instincts as you work and perform. In the end, your creative instinct is your guardian angel, the only one you can trust.

32

DRESS REHEARSALS

Three dress rehearsals are desirable. The last dress rehearsal can be a preview performance. By this time, you should know what you are about. You should be secure in the role. All the hard work is behind you. The joy of creation lies ahead of you. You have approached the role as an artist; you have created a character.

These bits of advice will help you during dress rehearsals.

- If your curtain is 8:30 p.m., complete dinner by 5 p.m.
- Take a nap sometime in the afternoon.
- Get to the theatre in plenty of time.
- Do not rush into costume and makeup. Remember Salvini. Take your time.
- Conserve your energy in the dressing room.
- Visit the stage at least once before 7:30 p.m.

Stanislavsky says, "Never come into the theatre with mud on your feet. Leave your dust and dirt outside. Check your little worries, squabbles, petty difficulties with your outside clothing – all the things that ruin your life and draw your attention away from your art."[1]

Suddenly, your preparation for the first entrance looms large. Prior to your first entrance actors will be talking, stagehands will be busy working, costumers and makeup people will be making last-minute adjustments. It will be difficult to find a quiet corner to prepare. But you must prepare every night. It begins *before* your first entrance. It begins in your mind and heart and soul as you begin to apply your makeup, your costume. It begins as you enter the backstage area, sensing the overwhelming responsibility you have accepted: to create a human being on stage, someone different from you, unique, a special person. This is the magic and the craft of the actor.

The dress rehearsal provides an opportunity for the final touches prior to performance. A point here, a shading there, more eye makeup or less light. Delay the exit. Practise the curtain calls. Refine this moment. Brighten up this line. But everyone knows you are on the brink of opening night. The final polish will give a sheen to the play, but the test of an audience is the driving force at this time.

33

OPENING NIGHT

There is no escaping. You have arrived. And if you are nervous, that is expected. It will be a miserable day for you because – as you mumble with your friends, or try to hold a conversation with your parents, or try to eat lunch with your wife or husband – one consuming idea has enveloped you and it will not release you until you hear the roar of the audience.

But all the work has been completed. Since that first day, through the readings and blocking sessions and rehearsals and long hours of searching, experimenting, torturing over your role, you have been aiming for this day.

You have approached a role. You have built a step-by-step performance. You have a spine. You know your objectives. You know your actions. You have experienced your character during rehearsals. You have crossed the bridge from your own life into the life of this imaginary character.

Now go out and enjoy. And share that joy with those human beings in the audience. And remember: keep alive the desire to speak what you have to say, because only you can say it.

34

... AND BEYOND

In many ways, the real work of the actor begins after opening night. During the early stock company days and before the Actors' Equity Association was created to protect them, actors rarely were paid during the rehearsal period. The argument of the producers was simply that the actor didn't begin work until the audience arrived and besides, there was no revenue until the show was on.

That argument, of course, is tainted because we know that it is during the rehearsals that the performance is developed, but in many ways (no thanks to the old producers) the true task for the professional actor begins after the play opens. This task comes because now you are concerned with many new challenges.

Sustaining the performance

Every night and on matinees you must experience the entire role. Many times you may not feel like performing. Dinner didn't settle, you are preoccupied, you are emotionally disturbed, you are tired, some important news is forthcoming, etc. But you must direct your will to sustaining and experiencing the life of the character.

Adjusting to different audiences

Audiences do affect your playing. Some are boisterous; they will laugh and applaud at various times. You may have to wait for a laugh or hold for a reaction before resuming. Other audiences literally sit on their hands. You must not panic, but play the show fully, make your points, and trust the material.

Preparation for entry into scenes

Every night will be different. Some actors will tease you as you sit quietly and wait for your entrance. Others will annoy you if you suggest some kind of physical or character improvisation for preparation. Whatever you chose as your preparation, your fellow actors might not necessarily cooperate. They have their own way of working. That is why acting is so unique. If it works for you, do it regularly before each scene. If it be only a ten-second pause before entrance, do it every time.

New adjustments on stage

Things do happen on stage. Lines are dropped. Props are sometimes not in place. Actors do unusual things. Be prepared to adjust to happenings on stage. Keep your wits about you. Here are two personal examples of adjustments on stage.

I was playing Bernie Dodd, the young director in Clifford Odets's play *The Country Girl*, opposite Kim Stanley, a powerful actress. In Act 2, scene 1, I had a line: "You're as phoney to me as an opera soprano," after which Kim was to slap me. We rehearsed the slap so no one got hurt. But this one performance I was out of position and she whacked me on the side of my face, cuffing my ear. I heard a ringing noise in my head and suddenly I couldn't hear at all – I was deaf. For the rest of the scene I read Kim Stanley's lips. After the scene was over my hearing returned. I was sitting backstage when she approached me and said she thought that was the best that I had ever played that scene. And I said, "Thank you – *I was reading your lips the whole time!*"

I was playing Sitting Bull in the play *Indians* and had a long speech, demanding help from US government representatives. In the heat of passion – suddenly – I could not move my jaw. My jaw had locked. Instinctively I turned upstage with my back to the audience. I raised my arms high, as if I was praying. I worked my jaw until it unlocked and I was able to complete the scene. Later, some of my friends told me that they loved the show, especially the moment when I turned my back on the audience and went upstage. They assumed I was crying or praying as the character. I said, "Thank you – *I was just trying to unlock my jaw.*"

Keeping the illusion of the first time

The art of acting consists of recapturing and experiencing the essence of the play time after time as though it were happening for the first time. If your mind wanders, if you feel you've said these lines before, if the freshness is gone out of the performance, stop, select an object of concentration – a prop, a person, a piece of furniture. Now, listen to the lines fully; really concentrate on the words. Acting is listening and reacting. Just listen, then honestly react to what you hear and see. Try to capture the sense that you are hearing this line, seeing this person, saying these words *for the first time*. Remember, your line is dead until something clicks in you to give it life and meaning. That something is a *just-listened-to* moment, a realized discovery, a fresh accident. This now gives your line a new meaning and purpose and life.

Forget yesterday's performance, and zero in on now

"Gee, what a great show we had yesterday!" We've all said it. We've all said it and it has hung like an albatross around our necks and destroyed today's show. Nothing is as dead as yesterday's performance. Forget it. Start each performance anew, as if you never performed the play before.

Attack each scene and build on previous scenes

Try to find from the previous scene the spur for attacking the next scene. The emotional undercurrent, the humor, the purpose, the relationship, the hope, etc., usually is there for you to hang on to and take with you through the performance.

Don't stop to analyze a previous scene

It's human nature to want to go back and try to relive both good moments, to relish them, and bad moments, to find out what went wrong. But doing this as an actor in a performance risks you being unprepared for the scene coming up. You must resist this. Remember, the theatre is always *now* and the moment you experience this *now* is the entire play. This *now* dies the instant it is born, only to be reborn again and again. That is the magic of the theatre.

Finally, inspiration is a blessed thing. Some nights you will be inspired and the performance will take off: you will feel relaxed and every impulse will be wonderfully correct. If this happens, great – use it, enjoy it! But, it will not come all the time. Then you must use a system so your audience can see, understand, and appreciate the play.

This is the reason for your study and for this book. This is the reason for spelling it out, one-two-three, in steps you should take to touch your character, the actual, day-to-day things to do to help you develop a technique.

I may say, *play your action*; others may say, *you must believe*, or *you must do*, or *it is a gift given from God*, or *don't act, be*. The point is, if you have talent and desire for a life in the theatre and film, these steps will define, sharpen, complement, and further that talent.

A good actor is no accident. Actors are craftspeople. They know what they are doing and why. They know how to approach a role, and they know their *so therefores*. They are professionals in every meaning of the word, and their accomplishments in theatre and film have enriched all of our lives.

Part 4

STAGE VERSUS FILM

35

PROJECTING VERSUS BEING

It is not my intention to be comprehensive here on the differences between stage and film acting. This book has focused on acting for the stage. There are some excellent books on film acting, including the landmark books *Film Technique and Film Acting* by V. I. Pudovkin, and *The Film Experience: Elements of Motion Picture Art* by Roy Huss and Norman Silverstein. I also recommend Michael Caine's *Acting in Film: An Actor's Take on Moviemaking* and Peter Bogdanovich's *Pieces of Time: Peter Bogdanovich on the Movies*.

The stage actor *projects*. The film actor *is*. Here are some preliminary broad strokes painting the differences.

- Preparation: The stage actor has considerable time to prepare and can count on a rehearsal period. The film actor rarely gets sufficient rehearsal time.
- Continuity: The stage actor is working in the role from his or her page one to his or her final moment on stage. The film actor usually shoots out of sequence.
- Matching: The stage actor plays before different audiences. The performance may change slightly, but the actor experiences the entire arc of the character from beginning to end. The film actor must match his or her performance for the sake of the continuity of the film. His or her tone, physical actions, and dialogue spread out over a number of different shots or setups. He or she must be prepared to deliver several takes until the director is satisfied.
- Staying fresh: The stage actor begins the play in front of an audience that reacts: they may laugh; they may get very quiet

and listen. These reactions can be felt and heard by the actors onstage, which serves as instant feedback. For a film actor, the work happens in spurts, the audience is usually the working crew, led by the director, and there is a great deal of waiting for setups. The film actor must have the ability to stay relaxed, to repeat, and to create the illusion of the first time repeatedly and quickly.

• Response: The stage actor knows immediately how an audience is responding to his or her work. The film actor must wait a long period of time until the film is finally completed and then released before he or she gets audience reaction.

36

THE SCENE VERSUS THE SHOT

Based on my personal observations over the years, it appears that many young actors prefer to work in film and television. There are more opportunities for them and thus this becomes their preferred goal. So therefore, when students ask, "What is the difference between acting for the stage and acting on film and in television?" I respond with specifics.

First, on the stage we act larger than life. In approaching the play, the actor is concerned with projecting the performance. That is, the voice should be stronger and the movements clearer than life so that the folks in the balcony can hear every word and follow the story. And the rehearsal schedule is long enough to allow the actor to become comfortable and secure in the role.

When the actor moves into film and television, things are quite different. It has been said that in the theatre, you have to *act*, but on film, you have to *be*. The camera brings you close to the audience and the microphone makes it easy to understand what the actor is saying. There is no need to project. There is no audience. There is only you, the other actors, the director, and the camera. (The exceptions to this rule are television shows that are filmed in front of a live audience, sometimes with as many as four cameras.)

The language and the techniques of film are rarely based on the scene. It is the shot which is the currency of film. A shot is dictated by where the director and cinematographer (also called the director of photography or DP) decide to place the camera (this is the camera angle or setup which creates the point of view for the eventual audience). A scene is then usually put together by the editor from several of these shots.

Michelangelo Antonioni, the director of such films as *Blow-Up*, *La Notte*, and *L'Avventura*, felt that each camera setup was a moral decision. I take that to mean that it is through the choice of camera setups, angles, and the use of different lenses that he introduces us to the characters, their conflicts, and their lives. Like a painter selecting the proper colors and shading for his canvas, these shots or setups, when put together, must illuminate and clarify the story that the director is trying to share with us.

A scene may be shot in many different ways. Usually the master shot comes first, in which the entire scene is shot. Here the events unfolding within the scene will happen in chronological order, as in a stage play scene. Usually all of the actors, including both the principals and the background artists (if they have action in the particular scene), are involved in the shooting of that master shot. Often, the master shot is a wide-angle shot encompassing the whole of the action from a distance with enough perspective to include, or at least indicate, where all the action takes place.

After this, the director will begin shooting coverage of the same scene from different angles. Perhaps a two-shot (the camera moves closer and covers the action between two characters), or an over-the-shoulder (the camera moves behind the shoulder of one character to film another character who is interacting with the first character), or a shot over the top (sometimes called an aerial shot), or from the bottom, at foot-traffic level. There are a myriad of shots from which the director and cinematographer can choose, including dolly shots (from a camera mounted on a moving dolly and moving either with the action or sometimes as counterpoint to the action) and handheld shots (where the camera is carried to the action, allowing for coverage from many angles in a single shot). Finally, the director will usually shoot a series of close-ups of the actors.

At either the end of the day or the next day, the director, producer, and editor will look at the day's work (called the rushes or dailies). Sometimes, the director will want to reshoot a scene or add another scene, feeling that perhaps he or she didn't get all of the required shots to tell the story.

A film is a picture puzzle; each piece must fit neatly into the whole so that the final picture represents the vision that the director is trying to create. The director and the editor are really the composers of the film. Their judgment as to which shots to use to create the final product is the crucial element in the success of their storytelling.

But let's get back to the work of the scene. The actor, during the different pieces of coverage, has the same lines, the same business, and the same objective and actions to play. The actor must match exactly what he or she did in the master shot. The actor should always know where the camera is and which light is his or hers. And, in the close-up, the actor must learn how to keep it real and simple.

For live television, with an audience close to you and three or four cameras to deal with, the actor must especially focus on staying in the moment and using his or her powers of concentration to filter out distractions.

Whether you are working in a play, a film, or a television show, I believe the actor should study the entire script. That will answer many questions for you (such as your purpose in the story and your relationship to the other characters) and, above all, provide a clear map as you explore your scenes, your actions, your objective, and your character. I realize that sometimes you will not be given the entire script. You may only receive sides (pages that include your cues and your lines). Situation comedies on television usually have a cast read-through on the first day, during which you can take notes. However, especially in television, you have to contend with a constant revision process: one day your scene may be in, the next day out or radically different. You have to make the adjustments. In all cases, try to get the whole script if at all possible. Then you will be able to do your homework.

In filmmaking, especially, a character is developed piecemeal and each piece must follow logically from the previous one. If a film is a picture puzzle, the puzzle cannot be complete without each piece. So therefore, each piece of that puzzle is significant. All the pieces are numbered. Even in a short television show, scripts contain several scenes. Though you may only appear in a few scenes, your role matters. Edward G. Robinson once said:

> I think the actors who endure are those who feel a responsibility to the character they play. Your role is another human being to

whom you owe your full attention and respect. You can't allow yourself to get in the way of that character. Any number of actors allow themselves to become more important than what they are doing. This is not right. There's no such thing as a little role or a big role. Even if the character has only one line, you must remember, you're doing a human being.[1]

Let us say that you appear in just three scenes: scenes 11, 72 and 93. Now, unlike in a play, which you study and learn from beginning to end, in a film rarely will scenes be shot in sequence. There are issues of weather, light, schedules involving set and locations, actors' schedules, and technical considerations that force out-of-sequence shooting.

Suppose the assistant director (usually the second assistant director, often called the second AD) calls you the night before you are scheduled to begin and says, "We are starting tomorrow morning at 6:00 a.m. with your scene 72," but you have studied and prepared scene 11.

If you have worked on the entire script, you have broken down the scenes in terms of actions and objectives and *as ifs*, and perhaps even a personal connection. You would also be aware of how scene 72 should begin for you. *So therefore*, based on what you had planned to do with scene 11, what you do *now* in scene 72 should be logical and consistent with your entire character. Also, ask yourself crucial questions, such as:

- What are the time and emotional connections between scene 11 and scene 72?
- How will you prepare for each scene?
- How will you approach scene 93?
- Will you have changed?
- What is the time difference between scenes?
- If this is your last scene, does it satisfy the story and the director's intentions for the story, as well as your own for the character?

Having studied the script, you will know your purpose in the story, and your actions and objectives will guide you. And, if the director wants to try different approaches to your character, you will be secure enough to do it.

Many actors today insist on rehearsing the film script, beginning at least with a table read, before the actual shooting begins. This helps them to digest the vision of the screenwriter. The collaboration of the writer, director, and actor is richer for everyone concerned.

Matt Damon, in an interview with *Entertainment Weekly*, spoke of his frustration during the filming of *The Bourne Ultimatum* in which he starred. He said, "In any given scene I didn't know where I'd just come from or where I was going. Which, as an actor, you kind of need!"[2] I would add, you certainly do!

My son, Michael Ruscio, a fantastic film editor and director, offers this advice:

> Because of the nature of filmmaking, anything can and will happen. Even the smallest role, a supporting actor, may find him or herself on screen for a reaction, a cutaway for a reason that may not seem apparent on the set. So therefore, at all times, the actor needs to listen, to react truthfully. An actor never knows how his/ her performance will be used in the final cut.[3]
>
> About matching, part of the craft of acting is to repeat. But I'm not just talking about the mechanics of matching, I'm talking about the ability to match the intent of the scene, be it on take one or take eight, and there is always room for reinterpretation or variation within that matching.

Keep it simple. Be real. Listen.

I've learned some basic truths about film acting: keep it simple; be real; listen; react truthfully; don't overact; and, listen to your director.

- Years ago, I toured with Steve McQueen in a play called *A Hatful of Rain* by Michael Gazzo. Kim Hunter and Nick Colasanto were also in the cast. It was a wonderful experience. The only sour note was that the stage manager kept telling McQueen that he must speak up during the play. Steve just laughed it off. He said he was uncomfortable projecting; he just wanted to be himself. Years later, when Steve McQueen moved into television and film his *just being himself* made him a star. The camera caught his special quality. It was always there, but on film he could share it with the audience.

- One of my early jobs on television was *The Untouchables*, with Robert Stack in an episode titled "The Artichoke King." My character had just gotten rid of the owner of a store and now I was enjoying my victory as I entered the store for the first time. The director, Bernard Kowalski, wanted me to sit at the desk and look around the room. I argued with him saying, "I want to walk around the room and gloat over my conquest." But he said, "If you are sitting down, I can put you into a close-up: we can see your eyes, your smile and your arrogance. Plus, with music in the background, we will really establish your character."[4] He convinced me, and he was right.

- In another early television role, I was on *Gunsmoke*. My scene was to enter the room, confront James Arness (Marshal Dillon), and say, "Do you want to see me?" Richard Whorf was the director. He was a wonderful actor and now he was directing. I thought I could impress him with this scene. I came into the room, and yelled out my line. Mr. Whorf said, "Cut!" He called me aside and said, "Are you from New York?" I answered, "Yes," and he said, "Look, in this scene, you are playing a cowboy; you care about your horse, and your land, and your cattle. Just keep it simple."[5] And he was right.

37

OPPOSING VIEWS

Here are two opposing and important ways to view the subject of stage versus film acting.

In his book *A Life,* Elia Kazan, the renowned film and stage director, describes how when he first went to Hollywood to make movies he met the film actor George Raft, and how Raft explained the difference between stage and film acting.

> First of all, on the stage you have to talk, right? But here, it's pictures. The less you say, the better. Get rid of as many lines as you can. Give them to the other guy. Let him tell the story and so on. You just look at him, sort of doubting what he says. Everybody in the audience will be wondering what you're thinking. In the picture business, wondering is better than knowing.[1]

By contrast, in his book *Pieces of Time,* Peter Bogdanovich writes about Orson Welles's reaction to James Cagney's performance in the film *White Heat* and the absurdity of all the writings about the difference between movie acting and stage acting. Bogdanovich quotes Welles as saying:

> Look at Cagney: everything is big and yet it's never for a moment unbelievable. It's true. He's a great movie actor and his performances are in no way modulated for the camera; he never scaled anything down.[2]

The same can probably be said for Orson Welles himself, along with Bette Davis, Joan Crawford, John Wayne, Gregory Peck, and a whole host of movie greats.

There was a time when the "legitimate theatre", as it was called, represented the epitome of the art of acting. In the 1930s and 1940s, some actors from the famous Group Theatre in New York City deserted the ship to venture west to Hollywood for film and big money. Actors like John Garfield and Franchot Tone were considered traitors who left the real theatre. Film was new and considered inferior to acting on the stage.

Today, however, actors move comfortably between stage and film. These venues complement each other. Jessica Lange, Gene Hackman, Dustin Hoffman, Helen Mirren, Denzel Washington, Judi Dench, Anthony Hopkins, Al Pacino, and many, many others all began their careers on stage and became Hollywood film stars. In fact, Hollywood producers and casting directors now regularly attend plays in New York and across the country seeking new faces for the film industry. There is a happy marriage between the legitimate theatre and the film industry. And the movement goes both ways. For example, a very successful film, *The Producers*, was transferred to the New York stage and became an enormous hit for the legitimate theatre.

Ultimately, the actor is the one who benefits from this movement because the actor learns the techniques necessary for all the venues: stage, film, and television. And, today, unlike in the old days, the trained actor can make a handsome living practising his or her craft.

Four helpful observations

1   If they call you for a 6:00 p.m. shoot on location, get plenty of sleep, because they may not get to your scene until 3:00 a.m.
2   If you are doing a sitcom in front of a large audience, play off your fellow actors. Acknowledge the audience (hold for a laugh, etc.) but play to your fellow actors as you rehearsed it.
3   Always be prepared for new lines at any time. If you are secure in your character, you should do fine.
4   Above all, be grateful that you are working in your chosen profession. And, during that brief time, you are creating magic and joy for an audience.

Part 5

STAMINA, LUCK, AND CHUTZPAH, AND OTHER LESSONS

38

STAMINA, LUCK, AND CHUTZPAH

All of the experiences I relate here really did happen to me. They are all true. At the times they happened I was not thinking of stamina or luck or chutzpah; I was merely trying to survive and get work as an actor.

"Something's gone wrong"

On the television show called *You are There* I was an extra, playing a radio operator during the Hindenburg disaster. The director, Sidney Lumet, encouraged all of us *to be real*. In the rehearsal I got caught up in the excitement and mumbled the words, "Something's gone wrong." Lumet said, "What did you say?" I repeated the line. He said, "Keep it in."[1] And that was how I got my first speaking role on television.

The old blue suit

I was in college and wanted to take part in an open call for actors to appear in a movie with Jimmy Cagney. I overslept so I didn't have time to shave. I threw on my old blue suit and rushed down to the Fairmont Copley Plaza Hotel. Around 500 guys showed up. Henry Hathaway, the director, announced they were looking for men to play OSS men in this movie called *13 Rue Madeleine*. Hathaway walked around the room picking out his cast. He pointed in my general direction and said, "You, the guy in the old blue suit who needs a shave."[2] I got the part.

Kim Hunter

One of the first shows I did in California was *Zorro* at Disney Studios. I met the director, Robert Altman, who looked at my résumé and saw that I had toured with Steve McQueen and Kim Hunter in *A Hatful of Rain*. He asked me about Kim Hunter. We spent about twenty minutes talking about Kim Hunter. Finally he said, "Thank you" and I headed toward the door. I turned back, and he said, "Oh, by the way, you got the part."[3]

"Are you the guy for the part?"

I read in the *Hollywood Reporter* that Allied Artists was about to begin a picture called *Al Capone* starring Rod Steiger. I had no agent and I didn't even know where Allied Artists was. I just got into my old car and drove around until I found Allied Artists on Sunset Boulevard. I arrived very early and went up to the office. The secretary said, "Are you the guy for the part?" I didn't hesitate for a second: I answered "Yes." It seemed like she was expecting someone, but I was the guy who was *there*. She led me into a room where I met two producers and the director. They asked me to, "Stand up and turn around." Then they handed me a script and asked, "Could you start tomorrow morning?"[4] I said, "Yes." I worked on the film for three and a half weeks, got myself an agent, and my Hollywood career began to take off.

"Now I'm ready"

My first television series as a regular was called *Shannon*. It was on CBS and starred Kevin Dobson. I played his father-in-law, a fisherman. We shot it in San Francisco. The final audition was at CBS Studios in Hollywood. When they called my name I walked into the room. It was very dark. I could hear voices coming from the seats in front of me. Then I heard a voice say, "Are you ready?" I answered in a loud voice, "No!" There was much mumbling coming from the seats. Then I took a deep breath, took time to remember my preparation for the scene, and, finally, I said, "Now I'm ready." I got the part.

The winter coat

Winters are cold in New York. One winter I was on the verge of catching pneumonia, so I took the bus back to my home town to visit my family. My two sisters, Dora and Flora (honest), insisted they buy me a new winter coat. I resisted and then I went along with it. They found a beautiful black coat with fur lining that really kept me warm. After a few days I returned to New York. I had an audition at CBS. As I entered the room, the casting director said, "That's a great coat." I explained that my sisters bought it for me as a Christmas present. He asked about my family. We talked for several minutes. Then he read me for the part. As I was about to leave he said, "You got the part." And he added, "You know why?" Before I could answer he said, "Because you didn't ask for it." Then he added, "You got a wonderful family – take care of that coat."[5]

"Mr. Coppola wants you in the picture"

My agent got me a reading for a role in *Godfather III*. I was to meet the director Francis Ford Coppola at 6 p.m. at a studio in Hollywood. I explained that I was doing a play and had to be at the theatre by 7 p.m. So I showed up at 6 p.m. and Fred Roos, one of the producers, was there. By 6:30 I was getting a little concerned. And by 7 p.m. I had to leave. A few days later, my agent called and said, "Mr. Coppola wants to meet you; same time, same place." I got there. Fred Roos was there. But no Coppola. At 7 p.m. I again had to leave. A few more days passed and my agent called and said the same thing: "Mr. Coppola would like to meet you at 6 p.m.; same place. So I showed up again: 6 p.m.: no Coppola; 6:30 p.m.: no Coppola; 7 p.m.: no Coppola. Now I was getting a little upset. I got up to leave and Fred Roos said, "Al, I have a camera here, why don't you talk to the camera and I will see that Mr. Coppola sees the tape?" And I said, "I don't know; I'm pretty upset." And Fred said. "That's all right. Just be yourself. Say whatever you want." So … I let Coppola have it. I insulted Francis Ford Coppola. I let it all out. I even cursed him in Italian. And I walked away with the satisfaction of having been honest. I figured I would never meet the man, and of course it was goodbye to my chances of being in *Godfather III*.

A few days later my agent called and said, "Mr. Coppola wants you in the picture."[6] I worked five weeks on the movie, shooting in Rome. It was a fantastic experience. Mr. Coppola saw something in my anger that he liked. And I learned that you must always be honest.

So therefore, you never know what the next day will bring. Be ready. Get to that appointment on time (early is better). Keep your wits about you. Never give up. Luck comes to those who are prepared.

I am reminded of an old quote, "Work hard; earn more than you are getting, and some day someone will pay a premium for your knowledge."

39

REMEMBERING LEAR

Figure 8 Al in *King Lear* as the regal monarch. (Photograph: gift of Robert G. Egan)

The year 1994 began as a disaster for me and my family. First, we experienced a terrible earthquake in our neighborhood which destroyed many homes and took many lives. Then we lost our beautiful granddaughter, Nydia. She was born with a heart defect and died at nineteen weeks. Then my good friend and theatrical agent Len Kaplan died of a heart attack. And at the end of May, my mother Nicoletta died. I flew back to Massachusetts and, on my birthday, June 2nd, we buried my mother.

In the middle of June I received a wonderful note of sympathy from my friend and director, Robert G. Egan. He and I had enjoyed a tremendous success with our production of *The Man in the Glass Booth* in Los Angeles. He had also persuaded me to play Shylock in *The Merchant of Venice* a few years after that. Now he was asking me to begin work on one of the greatest roles in history: King Lear. He said, "It is given to the actor to share their experiences for the greater illumination of art."[1]

I came to realize that the actor's tools are forged from the human experience; that the people we know and love who leave us also leave us a heritage of a richer appreciation of life, and through art and drama we can share that knowledge for a greater communal purpose.

I remembered Olivier's advice: "When you've the strength for it, you're too young; but when you've the age, you're too old."[2] But Bob Egan reminded me that I was now at just the right age: old enough to have the wisdom and still young enough to have the energy. Bob persuaded me. And so we decided to try to climb Mt. Everest and attempt *King Lear*.

We approached the play with the main idea that the king, at the beginning, was like the Old Testament God, Jehovah, whose strength and power ruled the world. But through suffering and madness and knowledge and humility, he becomes the New Testament God, Jesus, the God of love and charity and consideration and kindness.

We studied other versions of *King Lear*, including the Japanese *Ran* by Akira Kurosawa. And we studied Stanislavski when he speaks of the Italian invasion of Russia by Eleanora Duse and Tommaso Salvini, extolling their passion and their realism.

When I was at the Neighborhood Playhouse, Sandy Meisner used to call me *Salvini* when I acted well. Now I had the opportunity to study this great Italian tragic actor. He and Adelaide Ristori and

Eleanora Duse toured Europe and Russia at the end of the nineteenth century. Ristori was a great Lady Macbeth, Duse was wonderful in everything, and Salvini was brilliant as Othello, Macbeth, and King Lear. Stanislavski praised both their talent and their intensity.

In my research I came across a wonderful book by Robert Lewis called *Advice to the Players* in which he states, "We study the great artists, try to understand what they do, and then set about formulating techniques to help us to those ends."[3] Lewis speaks of the "Italian invasion" of Russia and suggests that Stanislavski probably said to himself, "What are they doing that we are not?" Lewis goes on to speak of Anton Chekhov who, after seeing Duse act in *Antony and Cleopatra*, wrote to his sister, "While I was watching Duse, I realized why one is bored at the theatre in Russia."[4]

In *Some Views on Acting* Salvini says:

> I believe that every great actor ought to be, and is, moved by the emotion he portrays; that not only must he feel this emotion once or twice, or when he is studying the part, but that he must feel it in a greater or less degree – and to just that degree will he move the hearts of his audiences – whenever he plays the part, be it once or a thousand times.[5]

With Salvini as my guide, I plunged into the study of *King Lear*. Bob, my director, was extraordinarily helpful. He was patient: he knew this play; this was his dream – to direct *King Lear*. He would come to my home or I to his, and we would marinate in the play. Incidentally, "to marinate" was a favorite expression of his. To marinate meant to go over every line and nuance of the text. We spent hours going over every possible meaning of a line or its subtext. It was agony, joy, exhausting, and creative, all in one package.

The company of players was all excited. And then, finally, after several weeks of preparation, we opened on the grand stage of the Hatlen Theatre in Santa Barbara, located on the campus of the University of California, known as UCSB.

The reviews we received were excellent. Philip Brandes wrote that it was, "quite simply the finest production of this play I've seen in all my days as a reviewer. And Al Ruscio gives a mesmerizing performance."[6] And, for the *Los Angeles Times*, Brandes wrote:

You couldn't ask for a more lucid, insightful and impeccably realized staging of Shakespeare's greatest tragedy than director Robert G. Egan's inspired production. ... The role of Lear is the supreme test of a mature actor's craft, and guest artist, Al Ruscio, a familiar face from film and television, rises magnificently to the challenge.[7]

But the note that really meant the most to me was written by my director.

Dear Al:

I remember standing on your doorstep halfway through the summer – after one of those wonderful afternoon sessions we spent marinating in the play – and I recall saying then, that we would look back on that pleasure with great nostalgia someday. Another thought I had – and I expect you did too – was to wonder how we would look back on the actual work and final outcome of the production itself. Well, I guess we're still a little close to the moment to tell; when you've climbed Mt. Everest and planted the flag, the air's a little thin on the summit. It's dizzying. But, Jesus Christ, Al, we got here. We did it. We won. Whatever else I'll feel in the future, I'm pretty sure I will look back on this show as my best work as a director.[8]

Robert G. Egan

For all of my life, I will be forever indebted to Bob Egan. He made the entire experience of *King Lear* an once-in-a-lifetime joy. He did a fantastic job of analyzing and directing this most complex play. His dream came true. He managed to work with dozens of actors, some professionals, some amateurs, some students, and he put it all together into a delicious and fantastic theatre experience.

And, of course, I thank my Italian friend, Tommaso Salvini, that great actor, for his words that motivated me and for his life's work that inspired me.

Figure 9 Al as the broken king in *King Lear*. (Photograph: gift of Robert G. Egan)

40

THE SEMI-FINAL LESSON

As we near the end of this book, I want to thank two special men, John Tellier and Delbert Moyer Staley, who began my career. They taught me to speak, to not be afraid. Where I grew up, most of the guys went into the leather factory. These teachers gave me the courage that I could, one day, go to college and make something of my life.

When I was fifteen years old and a junior at Salem High School in Massachusetts, I met a teacher who saved my life. His name was John Tellier and he taught English, which I loved, and speech, which I hated.

I loved words and I loved to write. But to get up in front of my classmates was a terrifying experience. I was afraid; I couldn't focus. It seemed as though everyone was laughing at me.

One day Mr. Tellier asked me to stay after class. When all the other students had left, he said, "You are thinking about yourself. All the energy is going inside of you – not out, where it belongs in order to communicate. Your energy must go outside of you, into the people you are talking to. Once you allow your energy to go out to the audience, you will stop being afraid, you will forget about yourself and focus on what you are trying to say."

And then he said, "So, what do you think will happen if you do that?"

I said, "If I could do that – really concentrate on what I was saying and trying to express, without being afraid or thinking about myself, so that people would really listen to me and we could share a moment together – wow! –that would be terrific."

And he said, "You can do it, young man."[1]

He worked with me. Gave me speech exercises. We read poetry aloud. We worked on correct breathing and articulation. He gave me confidence. He even got me a small role in the drama department's play called *The Bracelet of Doom*. And he helped me earn a scholarship to college.

Since that precious time many years ago, I have had a successful acting career and written books and articles. I have taught in theatre schools, universities, and movie studios. I believe that teaching is a glorious profession that helps young men and women grow and become proud and happy and prosperous and generous citizens. One teacher can make all the difference. One teacher can make you realize your potential and make you reach for heights that you never dreamed of. It happened to me, thanks to my teacher, John Tellier.

Delbert Moyer Staley was an actor who loved to teach. His specialty was speech. He met a politician named James Michael Curley. Curley said, "If you teach me how to speak, I promise you, I will help you."[2]

Curley became a great orator and when he was elected mayor of Boston, he gave Dr. Staley a license to open a school. The school was called Staley College of the Spoken Word. When I was seventeen years old I won a scholarship to Staley College. I met Mayor Curley and was mesmerized by his voice and strength and magic when he spoke. He openly admitted that Dr. Staley had taught him "how to use his voice."

Staley worked on diaphragmatic breathing. We did all kinds of exercises. Our voices were continually being tested. Slowly, we could feel the power of trained voices building inside us. How to hold a note. When to pause. The three volumes: high, conversational, and low. Like music. And we worked on different kinds of speeches and movement.

After World War II, I returned to Staley. Now 22 years of age, I became one of his favorite students. He asked me to assist in his classes. Then he invited me to teach my own class. Every Monday evening I taught a group of professional men and women: doctors, lawyers, politicians, priests, ministers, rabbis, etc.

They would get up and I would slowly take them through voice exercises and movement to dramatize their speech. We used a text called *The Psychology of the Spoken Word*. It was written by Dr. Staley and included all kinds of speeches and exercises. Then I would share with my class a secret I learned from Staley. Whenever he had to deliver a speech extemporaneously, he used a formula.

He used the word "P-R-I-E-S-T" to guide him into a speech on any subject. For example, the *P* could stand for People, the *R* for Recently, the *I* for Incidentally, the *E* for Economics, the *S* for Society, and the *T* for Therefore.

Try this exercise on any subject. You'll be surprised how it helps you to keep on your subject, and how each speech has a beginning, a middle, and an end.

To this day, I keep Dr. Staley's book near my desk to review some of the great ideas that he espoused. For instance, in the section *Pitch* he offers this fascinating notion:

> Every idea awakens a peculiar feeling of its own and the voice naturally will respond in different keys; as, for instance, in a degree of sorrow or melancholy, the voice will have a minor key; while in love, it will be a major key; also in joy. In other words, every idea, if truthfully enjoyed and lived, will have a key of its own and the voice will respond in these various keys, thus revealing the grasp of the mind on each successive idea.[3]

And in the section *Memorizing* he states, "endeavor to know what each idea means and how it leads into the next idea."[4]

And, in relation to playing a character, "My earnest advice is to BE, not to DO the thing, and in order to BE, it is necessary for you to live and become the very character you wish to impersonate."[5]

I am eternally grateful for having met and worked with these two teachers, great-hearted and inspirational men who gave me the courage to act and the opportunity to teach.

41

THE FINAL LESSON

I have been an actor, director, and teacher all of my adult life. In my classes one student inevitably asks the question, "How do you get started in this profession?"

I usually answer with a quote by Sandy Meisner, who, in addressing our freshman class at the Neighborhood Playhouse School of the Theatre, many years ago, said:

> It takes twenty years to become an actor. And, in a class of fifty students, perhaps one or two of you will still be working as actors in that period of time.[1]

During that time you will be testing your talent on a variety of plays and films and television programs that await you. You will also be seeing plays and studying good actors and you will appear in little theatres and large theatres, playing a variety of roles, all the time perfecting your craft.

Then I usually quote Sir Laurence Olivier: "To succeed as an actor you must have the strength, the will, and the determination of an ox."[2]

And that's a pretty good formula whether you are an actor or a doctor or a teacher or in any other profession where you hope to succeed.

The French writer Voltaire said, "You must have the Devil in your flesh [*le diable au corps*] to excel in all the arts."[3] I don't know about that, but I do know that you must have complete commitment to the craft and total love for the work.

The most direct answer that I can give to the question, "How do you get started?" is simple: just start. No matter where you are, find a theatre, volunteer to work, learn all you can about the life of the actor and the theatre. Get your feet wet, find a good teacher, study; you will soon discover if this life is for you. Just start. Get the taste and smell of acting. It's either in your blood or it's not. You will know – when and if you are ready.

And, to all actors: never be afraid or ashamed of any odd jobs you may undertake as you are trying to get your career started. These jobs serve a vital function. They awaken your powers of observation and enhance your skills because you will meet different kinds of people in all kinds of situations, and, if your eyes are open and your senses alert, they will give you a free acting education.

Finally, I hope this book has provided you with a truly practical guide as you develop your talent. All of these lessons and exercises have proven beneficial during my long and successful career.

So therefore, good luck to you in all your endeavors as you venture forth, seeking the fabulous rewards of the life of an actor.

NOTES

Preface

1 Odets, C. (1935) *'Golden Boy'*. In *Six Plays of Clifford Odets*. New York: Grove Weidenfeld, p. 252.
2 Masters, E. L. (1966) *Spoon River Anthology*. New York: Samuel French, p. 57.

About the author

1 Brandes, P. (1994) [theatre review of *King Lear*]. *Santa Barbara News-Press*, 20 October 1994.
2 Brandes, P. (1994) [theatre review of *King Lear*]. *The Los Angeles Times*, 20 October 1994.

2 Relaxation

1 Strasberg, L. (1953) 'Acting and Training of the Actor'. In Gassner, J. (ed.) *Producing the Play*. New York: Holt, Rinehart and Winston, pp. 128-162.

3 Concentration

1 Boleslavsky, R. (1933) *Acting: The First Six Lessons*. New York: Theatre Arts, p. 22.

4 Imagination

1 Stanislavski, C. (1936) *Creating a Role*. New York: Theatre Arts, p. 20.
2 Adler, S. (1988) *The Technique of Acting*. New York: Bantam Books, p. 17.
3 Moore, S. (1968) *Training an Actor*. New York: Viking, p. 15.

4   (The quote from Vittorio Mussolini was related to me by a producer of *Playhouse 90* in 1958 or 1959).

5 Beneath the words

1   Richardson, R. (1957) 'Acting Means Dreaming'. *The New York Times*, 10 February, 1957.
2   Corey, J. (late 1970s) (personal communication during Corey's acting class).

6 Sensory exercises

1   Meisner, S. (1987) *On Acting*. New York: Vintage, p. 16.
2   Aristotle. (1913) *On the Art of Poetry*. Translated by Lane Cooper. New York: Harcourt, Brace and Company, p. 24.

7 Improvisation

1   Stanislavski, C. (1936) *An Actor Prepares*. New York: Theatre Arts, p. 67.
2   Meisner, S. (1948) (personal communication in Meisner's acting class).
3   Fitzgerald, B. (1952) (personal communication on the set of *Lux Video Theatre*).

8 Animal studies

1   Olivier, L. (1994) *Confessions of an Actor*. London: Orion Paperbacks, pp. 154-155.

9 Life studies

1   Olivier, L. (1986) *On Acting*. New York: Simon and Schuster, p. 125.
2   Cole, T. and Krich Chinoy, H. (eds.) (1949) *Actors on Acting*. New York: Crown Publishers, p. 132.
3   Chaplin, C. (1949) 'The Study of Comedy'. In Cole, T. and Krich Chinoy, H. (eds.) *Actors on Acting*. New York: Crown Publishers, p. 523.

10 Emotional recall

1   Meisner, S. (1948) (This "quote" by Stanislavski has been repeated by noted acting teachers without any specific attribution for decades. I heard it from Sandy Meisner in his acting classes, beginning in 1948).
2   Gray, P. (1964) [Sandy Meisner in NY, 11 June 1964]. *Tulane Drama Review* 9 (2), Winter 1964.

12 The spine of the play

1   Clurman, H. (1953) 'Principles of Interpretation'. In Gassner, John (ed.) *Producing the Play*. New York: Holt, Reinhart and Winston, p. 277.
2   *Ibid.*
3   *Ibid.*
4   *Ibid.*
5   Boleslavsky, R. (1933) *Acting: The First Six Lessons*. New York: Theatre Arts, p. 62.

13 The spine of the character

1   Kazan, E. (1963) 'Notebook for *A Streetcar Named Desire*'. In Cole, T. and Krich Chinoy, H. (eds.) *Directors on Directing: A Sourcebook of the Modern Theatre*. Indianapolis: Bobbs-Merrill, pp. 364-379.

15 Your actions in the scene

1   Stanislavski, C. (1936) *Creating a Role*. New York: Theatre Arts, p. 20.
2   Saroyan, W. (1947) '*The Time of Your Life*'. In Gassner, J. (ed.) *Best Plays of the Modern American Theatre*. 2nd series. New York: Crown, p. 48.
3   Meisner, S. (1949) (personal communication in Meisner's acting class).
4   Boleslavsky, R. (1933) *Acting: The First Six Lessons*. New York: Theatre Arts, p. 67.

16 The *as if*

1   Meisner, S. (1948) (personal communication in Meisner's acting class).
2   Cole, T. and Krich Chinoy, H. (eds.) (1949) *Actors on Acting*. New York: Crown Publishers, p. 528.
3   Meisner, S. (1952) (personal communication during a class at the Neighborhood Playhouse School of the Theatre).

17 Preparation

1   Kopit, A. (1969) *Indians*. New York: Hill and Wang, p. 71.
2   Shakespeare, W. *Hamlet*, Act 3, scene 2.
3   Breslin, J. (1962) 'Bob Cousy: The Little Giant'. *Cavalier* 12 (104), pp. 16-18.

22 The climax

1   Miner, W. (1953) 'Directing the Play: The Complete Procedure'. In Gassner, J. (ed.) *Producing the Play*. New York: Holt, Rinehart and Winston, pp. 215-216.

26 Elements of characterization

1   Olivier, L. (1986) *On Acting*. New York: Simon and Schuster, p. 29.

27 The use of improvisation

1   Seward, A. (2010) (letter from Anne Seward to Al Ruscio).

28 Blocking sessions

1   Meisner, S. (1987) *On Acting*. New York: Vintage, p. 34.

29 Detailed work on each act

1   Olivier, L. (1986) *On Acting*. New York: Simon and Schuster, p. 83.

31 Final run-throughs

1   Meisner, S. (1948-1950) (personal communication in Meisner's acting classes).
2   Ruscio, M. (1980s) (personal communication).

32 Dress rehearsals

1   Stanislavski, C. (1949) *Building a Character*. New York: Theatre Arts, p. 244.

36 The scene versus the shot

1   Robinson, E.G. (1972) *The Detroit News*, 2 October 1972.
2   Nashawaty, C. (2007) 'The Strong Violent Type'. *Entertainment Weekly* [online]. <available from http://www.ew.com/ew/article/0,,20049809,00.html> [6 August 2007].
3   Ruscio, M. (2009) (letter to Al Ruscio).
4   Kowalski, B. (1962) (personal communication on the set of the episode "Element of Danger").
5   Whorf, R. (1959) (personal communication on the set of the episode "Letter of the Law").

37 Opposing views

1   Kazan, E. (1988) *A Life*. New York: Knopf, p. 184.
2   Bogdanovich, P. (1962) *Pieces of Time*. New York: Delta, p. 106.

38 Stamina, luck and chutzpah

1   Lumet, S. (1953) (personal communication).
2   Hathaway, H. (1947) (personal communication on the set of *13 Rue Madeleine*).
3   Altman, R. (1958) (personal communication on the set of an episode of *Zorro*, Los Angeles).
4   (personal communication from the casting director and producers at Allied Artists for the film *Al Capone*, Los Angeles, 1958).
5   (personal communication from casting director, New York, winter 1953).
6   Roos, F. and Kaplan, L. (1990) (personal communication, Los Angeles).

39 Remembering Lear

1   Egan, R. G. (1994) (personal communication).
2   Olivier, L. (1986) *On Acting*. New York: Simon and Schuster, p. 131.
3   Lewis, R. (1980) *Advice to the Players*. New York: Harper & Row, p. 53.
4   *Ibid.*
5   Salvini, T. (1949) 'Some Views on Acting'. In Cole, T. and Krich Chinoy, H. (eds.) *Actors on Acting*. New York: Crown Publishers, p. 408.
6   Brandes, P. (1994) [theatre review of *King Lear*]. *Santa Barbara News-Press*, 20 October 1994.
7   Brandes, P. (1994) [theatre review of *King Lear*]. *The Los Angeles Times*, 20 October 1994.
8   Egan, R. G. (1994) (letter to Al Ruscio).

40 The semi-final lesson

1   Tellier, J. (1939) (personal communications, Salem, Massachusetts).
2   Curley, J.M. (1940) (personal communication, Boston, Massachusetts).
3   Staley, D.M. (1951) *Psychology of the Spoken Word*. 8th ed. Dedham, MA: Transcript Press, p. 20.
4   *Ibid.*, p. 33.
5   *Ibid.*, p. 33.

41 The final lesson

1   Meisner, S. (1950) (personal communication during an acting class at the Neighborhood Playhouse School of the Theatre).
2   Olivier, L. (1986) *On Acting*. New York: Simon and Schuster, p. 63.
3   Arouet, F.M. (Voltaire) (1877) *Oeuvres Complètes*, v.2. Paris: Garnier Frères, p. 5.

REFERENCES

Adler, S. (1988) *The Technique of Acting*. New York: Bantam Books.

Aristotle. (1913) *On the Art of Poetry*. Translated by Lane Cooper. New York: Harcourt, Brace and Company.

Arouet, F. M. (Voltaire) (1877) *Oeuvres Complètes*, v.2. Paris: Garnier Frères.

Bogdanovich, P. (1962) *Pieces of Time: Peter Bogdanovich on the Movies*. New York: Delta.

Boleslavsky, R. (1933) *Acting: The First Six Lessons*. New York: Theatre Arts.

Brandes, P. (1994) [theatre review of *King Lear*]. *The Los Angeles Times*, 20 October 1994.

Breslin, J. (1962) 'Bob Cousy: The Little Giant'. *Cavalier* 12 (104), February 1962.

Caine, M. (1990) *Acting in Film: An Actor's Take on Moviemaking*. New York: Applause.

Chaplin, C. (1949) 'The Study of Comedy'. In Cole, T. and Krich Chinoy, H. (eds.) *Actors on Acting*. New York: Crown Publishers.

Clurman, H. (1953) 'Principles of Interpretation'. In Gassner, John (ed.) *Producing the Play*. New York: Holt, Reinhart and Winston.

Cole, T. and Krich Chinoy, H. (eds.) (1949) *Actors on Acting*. New York: Crown Publishers.

Cole, T. and Krich Chinoy, H. (eds.) (1963) *Directors on Directing: A Sourcebook of the Modern Theatre*. Indianapolis: Bobbs-Merrill.

Gassner, J. (ed.) (1953) *Producing the Play*. New York: Holt, Rinehart and Winston.

Gassner, J. (ed.) (1958) *Best Plays of the Modern American Theatre*. 2nd series. New York: Crown.

Gray, P. (1964) [Sandy Meisner in NY, 11 June 1964]. *Tulane Drama Review* 9 (2), Winter 1964.

Huss, R. and Silverstein, N. (1968) *The Film Experience: Elements of Motion Picture Art*. New York: Dell.

Kazan, E. (1963) 'Notebook for *A Streetcar Named Desire*'. In Cole, T. and Krich Chinoy, H. (eds.) *Directors on Directing: A Sourcebook of the Modern Theatre*. Indianapolis: Bobbs-Merrill.

Kazan, E. (1988) *A Life*. New York: Knopf.

Kopit, A. (1969) *Indians*. New York: Hill and Wang.

Lewis, R. (1980) *Advice to the Players*. New York: Harper & Row.

Masters, E. L. (1966) *Spoon River Anthology*. New York: Samuel French.

Meisner, S. (1987) *On Acting*. New York: Vintage.

Michaels, S. (1962) *Tchin-Tchin*. New York: Samuel French.

Miller, A. (1958) '*A View from the Bridge*'. In Gassner, J. (ed.) *Best Plays of the Modern American Theatre*. 2nd series. New York: Crown.

Miner, W. (1953) 'Directing the Play: The Complete Procedure'. In Gassner, J. (ed.) *Producing the Play*. New York: Holt, Rinehart and Winston.

Moore, S. (1968) *Training an Actor*. New York: Viking.

Nashawaty, C. (2007) 'The Strong Violent Type'. *Entertainment Weekly* Online. Available from http://www.ew.com/ew/article/0,, 20049809,00.html accessed 6 August 2007.

Odets, C. (1935) '*Golden Boy*'. In *Six Plays of Clifford Odets*. New York: Grove Weidenfeld.

Odets, C. (1949) *The Country Girl*. New York: Dramatists Play Service.

Olivier, L. (1986) *On Acting*. New York: Simon and Schuster.

Olivier, L. (1994) *Confessions of an Actor*. London: Orion Paperbacks.

Pudovkin, V. I. (1949) *Film Technique and Film Acting*. New York: Bonanza Books.

Richardson, R. (1957) 'Acting Means Dreaming'. *The New York Times*, 10 February 1957.

Robinson, E. G. (1972) *The Detroit News*, 2 October 1972.

Salvini, T. (1949) 'Some Views on Acting'. In Cole, T. and Krich Chinoy, H. (eds.) *Actors on Acting*. New York: Crown Publishers.

Saroyan, W. (1947) '*The Time of Your Life*'. In Gassner, J. (ed.) *Best Plays of the Modern American Theatre*. 2nd series. New York: Crown.

Shakespeare, W. *Hamlet*, Act 3, scene 2.

Staley, D. M. (1951) *Psychology of the Spoken Word*. 8th edn. Dedham, MA: Transcript Press.

Stanislavski, C. (1936) *An Actor Prepares*. New York: Theatre Arts.

Stanislavski, C. (1936) *Creating a Role*. New York: Theatre Arts.

Stanislavski, C. (1949) *Building a Character*. New York: Theatre Arts.

Strasberg, L. (1953) 'Acting and Training of the Actor'. In Gassner, J. (ed.) *Producing the Play*. New York: Holt, Rinehart and Winston.